GW00361792

Dive As Deep As You Dare

Published by KAB Publishing Feb 2011

This is a true reflection on 28 years spent diving in various locations with some interesting and charismatic people some names have been changed.

The Author asserts the right to be recognised as the Author of this work
daveb.bristol@gmail.com

© Copyright 2010

ISBN 978-0-9568115-0-9

Printed and bound in the UK by

Short Run Press Ltd Exeter Devon EX27LW

Preface

'Dive as Deep as you Dare' tells the story of Dave Blackmore who has spent the last 28 years diving all around the world. He takes you on an incredible diving adventure to some of the deepest wrecks both at home and abroad.

My journey begins in the early 80's when my passion for diving evolved from childhood holidays to the real thing.

The diving equipment and techniques back then were in their infancy and limited the dives available to me and my dive buddies. But it didn't stay that way for long.

During the mid/late 80's I was pushing the boundaries, diving classic shipwrecks like HMS Hampshire & Blue holes in Florida to name but a few.

Approaching the 90's mixed gas became available and led to some life changing/heart stopping moments, like the Malta episode.....

"Passing 50 metres, I felt absolutely fine. I was used to diving to those depths in the UK, where the water is dark and you would need a 50 watt torch just to see your dive gauges. In the time it took me to look left across to my dive buddy and then ahead and back to my dive computer, I was at 65 metres and I could feel the effects of nitrogen narcosis. My brain was in some sort of dull, lethargic, trance and I wondered how deep we might get before we stopped. Again, I glanced at my buddy next to me. I could hear the bubbles pouring from his Poseidon regulator. I focused back on my dive computer: 70 metres. I checked myself "Am I still comfortable at this depth?" I was undecided and I was now at 75 metres. There was no end to the sloping sea bed I was following. The sound of the exhaled air from the regulators was all I could focus on. That's it…. I slowed to a stop at 79 metres and stared blankly ahead realising I was in trouble"

But it all began many years before.......

Contents

Early days

Diving is one of those sports that people either love or hate, but like most things, you will never know if you just sit back and think about it.

As a young boy I was always fascinated with water; on it and in it. At nine years old, holidaying at Brean near Weston Super Mare, most of my entire holiday money was spent on underwater apparatus just as I had seen on Jacques Cousteau's programmes - mine just looked slightly different.

The snorkel was attached to the top of the mask and had a cage on the top that enclosed a ping pong ball. In theory, as the water rose up, the ping pong ball would rise and cover the open end of the snorkel tube and stop the water and air being drawn in. Needless to say, it was a complete failure. The mask was also a waste of space, it had large gaps around my face and the water leaked in all over the place causing water to go up my nose and in my eyes; this situation did not seem to afflict Jacques Cousteau and the Calipso team.

Over the next few years, I began to take a bigger interest in the underwater scene and was inspired by Blue Peter. They were heavily in to using washing up bottles for various homemade topical interests of the day; so what the heck, I found an empty fairy liquid bottle, tipped away the remains of another and set about building my own twin set.

Once the two bottles had been washed out, I screwed in a small bike tyre valve, pumped in some air and connected some fish tank air pipe. Of course it did'nt work, but it passed what otherwise could have been a boring Saturday morning. There was nothing else for it, if I really wanted to dive, it would take more than washing up bottles to achieve it and it would be later on in life and with proper diving equipment.

After leaving school, leaving home and getting married, I set out to find a diving club. Through the local council I had heard of a club who met up at a local swimming pool on Tuesday evenings, so that was that, I was going along the following week.

I arrived at Filwood pool at 7 pm and sought out the most approachable person I could find. The lucky one was a white haired man called Bill Flower. I introduced myself and we shook hands. He was with another guy called Mike, who was a lot younger than Bill but they were keen to run through some of the basics on diving and how easy it was to join the club.

The pool session ended and I was invited to come along to the dive club just off the Cumberland Basin. Once inside, sat up at the bar, they ran through the first steps in learning to dive and it all sounded achievable.

Bill Flower had been diving for many years and is very passionate about diving. I got to ask plenty of questions, you know the ones: How long can you stay down? How deep can you go? What's the deepest you have been? Will I get the bends? And of course, how expensive is it?

After 30 minutes or so I had decided to join up and get started; I had been waiting for 10 years to do this, there was not a moment to lose.

The 'A' test was the first step and I only needed basic equipment: snorkel, mask, fins and a weight belt. I thought I had better get some proper ones this time and headed off to the only local outdoor sports shop in Bristol, called Peter's. The older man behind the counter seemed to know his stuff and reminded me a bit of Jacques Cousteau. I tried out a few different masks and they fitted and stuck to my face like glue; it's all down to the suction and not a ping pong ball in sight. I could hardly wait to try out all my new equipment at the pool.

It was November 1982 and I was now a member of the British Sub Aqua Club, this club being the third one to be established in the UK. Wow, how cool is that?

The next Tuesday I arrived at the pool keen as mustard. Bill Batey was the club instructor and he was to become a great source of knowledge and enlightenment over the coming years of my diver training. Bill learnt to dive whilst in the Royal Air Force, when on his days off he would spear fish. From what he told me he was very accomplished at it, and from my memory, he was stationed in Malta; nice work if you can get it.

The A test was the first of the basic skills I needed to master in order to dive and progress this new sport. Weeks of pool training were required to learn various skills to a perfect standard and the sooner I got to grips with them, the quicker I could get on with the next set. The one I remember was the one length breath hold swim, followed by a one minute breath hold at the side of the pool. It was hard, but we all did it. Of course, practice and dedicated training will always put you in a good strong position to succeed.

The last of this test was carried out in open water, off the coast at Seaton in Devon. Armed with wetsuit, weight belt, snorkel, mask and fins we sped out in the club boat. I would be free diving down to a depth of 7 metres and then carrying out a simulated rescue and life saving of a fellow snorkel diver. This took the whole morning and by the time it was all done and dusted I can only say I was very pleased; now I could get on with the real thing.

Back in Bristol the following week, I scurried down to Peter's diving shop to top up my snorkel kit with the all important scuba equipment that would allow me to dive properly underwater. There was a choice of demand valves and cylinders but nothing like there is today.

The choice of the day was a US Divers Con Shelf demand valve, a Luxfer aluminium cylinder and an ABLJ buoyancy jacket shaped like a toilet seat that went around your neck; all state of the art at the time. All that was needed now was the skills to use them; more training!

Bill Batey began my pool training the very next Tuesday with a basic kit assembly and functions demonstration. He then took me to the shallow end to show me what it could do. With demand valve in my mouth, I knelt down and submerged my head under the water and breathed in. It was unbelievable; my mind was telling me I shouldn't be able to breathe under water but I was, and it was great. Within 15 minutes, I had my head around it and I was swimming down the pool to the deep end. There was a slight pressure on my ears but a quick yawning action, or pinch and slight blow of the nose soon sorted it out, just like on a plane when it takes off or descends to land.

There was a lot to master, both practical and theory. I had a book to guide me and I would need to learn it from cover to cover, but most of all understand it, if I was to make a good, safe diver and pass the various tests and exams.

Training was similar to the previous snorkel training, with some extra tasks involved like ditch and retrieve, air sharing with a dive buddy, the physics of diving and not to forget life saving skills.

Throughout the winter months I had been in training and my younger brother Mike had also joined the club and was only a few weeks behind me in his training. We were both very keen to make the first open water trip at Easter. The diving would be from Hope Cove and although I had never been there I had heard it was very good for shore diving.

My Brother Mike is ten years younger than me and was only just old enough to learn to dive in the pool. The previous week, whilst he was carrying out some pool training, his instructor held on to his regulator whilst they were air sharing in the deep end of the pool. It gave Mike a bit of a shock, but probably taught him a valuable lesson in self preservation: never let someone else hold your Demand Valve even when you are practicing life saving skills.

It was Easter 1983 and all the pool training was completed. There were just some open water skills that needed to be put in to practice and I had a new instructor, Bill Flower. I didn't know how old Bill was, but he had a head of white hair that made him look older than he probably was.

The weekend was a bank holiday and Bill had booked a caravan. We needed to get enough people in it so that it did'nt cost an arm and a leg. Due to my work load, my brother and I didn't get to the van until Good Friday, but we were there for breakfast. Surprised, I saw he had roped in a few barmaids from the pub we sometimes used called the Nova Scotia, down in the centre of Bristol. They were obviously along for the social side of the weekend of late nights and liberal eating and drinking that would be customary with many of the weekends away.

By 10ish a few more people had arrived and the caravan looked full. After breakfast, we loaded up the car and headed for Hope Cove. The weather was extraordinary for an early Easter, the sun was out and the temperature was in the 70s, not that it would make much difference to the water temperature.

I got in to my wetsuit; it was 14 mm thick and by the time I had the rest of my kit on I was boiling. The sooner I was in the water, the better. As we all waded in to the sea, I looked at the others and couldn't help but smile as we looked like a load of black seals struggling through the surf. As the water reached my chest and I started to get the weight off my back, the water

5

began to penetrate through my wetsuit. It was freezing cold and it took a few minutes for my body heat to warm the suit so I could focus on the dive ahead. Bill led the way and we both followed in a monkey see, monkey do, fashion. Although the skills I had learned in the pool were working, it was just as well as right here in the open sea there was a current and a slight swell. The visibility was at least 8 metres and although there was not a great deal of marine life at a depth of 6 metres, the colours of the rocks, sea weed and the general buzz of the dive turned out to be quite a rush.

After about 20 minutes I was cold again and so were my fellow divers. Although we had wetsuits, they were only a temporary barrier against the cold sea and we headed for the shore and clambered up the beach in to the warm sunshine. My first dive in the sea all went as planned.

We all lazed about in the warm sun and reflected on the dive and decided on the next one; it was to be another beach dive and very similar to this one, but it was irrelevant; we would have dived in a puddle if that's all we could have found. After getting our cylinders re-pumped I bumped in to some other members of the dive club and got to hear some stories about their dive that day and what they were planning for the afternoon. There was a man called John, one of Bill's friends, and his wetsuit had been made by himself some years before. Back in the day, you could send away your details and get the neoprene sent back all cut to size in kit form. All you needed to do was glue and tape the seams up. It all appeared to be done on the cheap, no one seemed to have loads of money, but that suited me fine because with a young family of my own, neither did I.

In the evening we met up in a local pub and there was talk on sunken treasure, ships wrecks and the obligatory food that divers dive for: scallops, crabs and flat fish; basically anything that was shiny or edible was fair game.

On the Sunday, Mike and I had to get going, there were things on back at home, but it had been a great few days and we had the whole summer ahead. Saying goodbye to the rest of the people in the caravan, we learnt that the two girls would also be heading home as there was a pub to run and time was short. They also enlightened us that it was not really so cold in the caravan that they needed to wear pyjamas and dressing gowns, it was just that one of the guys was a bit too amorous towards them. Shortly after that weekend they left the pub and we never saw them again, although we still spent many a Tuesday night drinking some fine ales and soaking up the sea faring atmosphere that you will still find in the Nova Scotia pub today.

I was now well on my way to my 3rd class diver qualification. At the time, I was restricted to 17 metres maximum depth and that limited me to the dive sites available. The club had an inflatable boat that we used to do most of the dives from. The older members seemed to favour Seaton near Lyme Regis as a launch site as the beach is made of shingle and quite steep. I arrived at 7.30 am, parked the car on the main road and joined the other members in sorting out the boat and engine. It took 8 of us to carry the boat to the water, then we got the engine on 2 scaffold poles and repeated the process. It was then back to the car to kit up and carry my weight belt, cylinder and remaining equipment down to the boat. By this time it was 10.45 am and I was half worn out. The engine eventually started and half of us got in and set off; the other half had to wait as there was not enough room in the boat.

We headed out to dive a reef and go scavenging for crustations. Visibility was not that good and we headed back after a few hours. Already it had been a long day and it seemed like a lot of hard work for a 20 minute dive. At the end of the day around 6.00 pm, we carried the boat engine and all our equipment back up the beach. Bloody Hell, there must be an easier way; oh yes, there was the marina and it had a slip just round the corner. There was only one small problem - it cost a bit of money. Well, what can I say? I never carried that boat or engine again; heck you could break your back! What were they thinking?

By October 1984 I was pretty dive fit and gaining experience all the way. No longer restricted to 18 metres and free of the dreaded club boat gymnastics across the beach, I booked myself on a hard boat dive that Keith had booked at a princely sum of £5.00 for a whole day's diving. All I had to do was walk on to the boat with my dive gear, kit up and go over the side.

Driving down to Swanage to dive the wreck of the *Kyarra,* a hospital ship torpedoed in 1918 sat in 30 metres of water, I was pretty keen to see what this wreck had to offer. After parking up on the pier, Mike and I wandered over to where the boat was moored up. It was an old wooden boat with a small wheel house and an open back. The skipper, Roger Wagstaff, was what you might call an old fisherman turned dive boat skipper and it didn't take long to realise this guy was a bit of a character with his wild side burns and short temper. To say he did not suffer fools gladly was an understatement; he was effing and blinding before we had even set foot on his boat let alone pissed him off.

We formed a chain and lowered the cylinders down to the boat with Roger watching and issuing instructions on where to put them all. The dive was very tide dependant and slack water was a must, not a preferred choice. Slack water only lasted 50 minutes then the tide would turn and the current would run like a train. If you found yourself in the water before or after slack water, you would find yourself half a mile from the wreck or dive boat in a very short time. Not a good place to be if you didn't want to be lost or another rescue statistic. I have been very fortunate in my 25 years diving never to have been lost at sea although I have known and met some less fortunate divers over the years. One particular diver springs to mind; he was lost for a couple of days but all credit to him and the two other divers he was with, all survived. However, only one continued to dive after that, but that's another story.

Once all the kit was on board, we got our wetsuits on and clambered aboard. With 12 divers and all their kit, there was not a great deal of room left on this small ex-fishing boat. However, the dive cost was kept to a minimum with the maximum amount of paying divers. The boat ride out to the wreck only took 20 minutes and about 10 minutes from the dive site the skipper hollered at us to get kitted up. His enthusiasm and lack of patience was evident with his determination that we should not miss slack water and the forthcoming dive, so we all needed to be in the water one pair after another.

The dive kit we used was pretty basic compared to what we tend to use now and as I remember, we all hit the water together as planned. Mike and I were diving together and dropped down the anchor line leading to the wreck. At about 22 metres we could see the wreck, the visibility was good and at 26 metres we landed on the wreck and set off through some large open parts of this old ship. Before long, I found a tile from the galley area and soon after, a bottle of something. With both now secure in my goodie bag, there was just time left to signal to Mike it was time to head for the surface in order to avoid the need for any decompression stops, as this was the plan prior to the dive.

Breaking through the surface we were met with bright sunshine and a calm sea. We spotted the dive boat not far away and with a few fin strokes we were back at the side of the boat and climbed up the ladder and in to the boat. Whilst the others were arriving back, I took a look at what I had found. The tile was not patterned and just had a cracked glaze but the bottle was full of something and the cork was still firmly in place. The rest of the divers were back on board and a few other people had the same bottles. We opened one and it went off with a pop. Fizzy liquid resembling Coca Cola foamed out of the neck and the skipper informed us it was Champagne, but it was far from drinkable, more's the pity. Nevertheless, it was a good dive and I would be back on this wreck again soon, as other, more experienced divers on the boat talked of further trips and forthcoming bookings.

The dive club is where most trips and plans were made and I had now been a member for 18 months. The membership was growing every week with people from all walks of life keen to learn to dive. No sooner had you got to know all the names and faces you had to remember some more.

As with many clubs it could have its separate groups and preferred conversational preferences; cliquey is a bit too strong a term to use. Having said that, every week, all dives were chalked up on the dive board and it was up to the individual to get his or her name up there pretty smart if they wanted to go on that dive and not end up on the reserve list.

There didn't ever seem to be a lack of things going on and Tuesday nights tended to turn in to a bit of a party. Most members, including myself, had a few drinks at the club bar and a few more just to support the club. Drinks were a bit cheaper than the local pub, but being purchased at the cash and carry there was a profit to be made and this was ploughed back in to the club account to pay towards various things like the club house compressor and boat to name but a few.

Some of the guys had been with the club from the start and tended to stick together. Nevertheless, there were plenty of new members now and I got along with most of them. We all progressed our social and diving skills as we went along, and after all these years, it's nice to say I am still in contact with some of them and we still manage to dive together on rare occasions.

As Seaton was a favoured place to dive, it's not a surprise that long weekends were planned at, or near that location. Camping was the choice of accommodation as most of the active dive members were well seasoned at either roughing it in a van or tent and the more you did it, the easer it got.

It was a typical weekend in the late 80s and Mike and I were at Seaton with 20 or so other people from the club. We were in the next bay along at Beer and had decided to go to a different pub. Bill Lewis had asked me to take his daughters in my car to the pub and told me they knew where it was. We headed off back to Seaton, parked up in the campsite field and walked to the pub. I told the girls to go straight in as Mike and I needed the loo. Standing at the urinals in the outside toilet - what a relief - we chatted and laughed about the day's antics. It's then that we realised that none of the urinals had plumbing attached to them and we had peed all over our feet. We were now in hysterics. It lent a whole different meaning to being on the piss.

We exited this so called loo to find the girls standing outside as we were, in fact, at the wrong pub. "So where is it?" we asked. They didn't think it was that far and would know it when they saw it. "That's great" I thought, but we were missing valuable drinking time and what would Bill be thinking? We had been gone nearly an hour. Ten minutes later we got to the right pub. Bill met us halfway across the bar with a relieved and stern look on his face. "Where have you been?" he asked. We told him and he saw the funny side, telling me I had just put my diving career back 10 years. My mate Dave Jeal told me he was asking whether the Blackmore brothers were OK and were his girls in honourable hands; "Of course" I replied, and we all had a good laugh. After 12 o'clock passed, I could see why they wanted to come here. My car was parked out in the pub car park and that's where it stayed. Mike and I staggered out and slept in it. By the time we felt human the next day, we had skipped the first dive and just completed the second one.

The second dive was a drift and we filled our goodie bags with scallops and plaice. Back at the campsite, we pooled our food resources and cooked it all up together. There were about 30 odd people by now and we were all fed well on the spoils of the sea with just a bit of help from 10lbs of potatoes and 2 dozen rolls. It's a great feeling when this many people all get on and pull together.

The following day was spent diving and generally chilling out. We had all decided to go to one pub and not surprisingly were unable to all get in to it, so we were split between the only two pubs in Seaton. After our food, we began to have a sing song in the pub. We were then asked to leave by a grumpy landlord so with drinks in hand we headed for the other pub where the landlord met us; "We have been barred" we told him, "What for?" he replied, "oh, singing" we told him. "You can sing all you like in my pub" he retorted, and that we did.

My good friend Andy Mawditt came up with a song and exercise routine called Sunshine Mountain. More and more people joined in, climbing up the climbing frame that was in the beer garden until it began to sink in to the ground. Still, we bought plenty of beer and food and the old landlord didn't seem to mind. We often revisited the pub, but kept off the climbing frame - we must have been getting older.

Hard Boats and dive crews

I was still with the same dive club in 1987, but had decided to organise some dive trips of my own and this would be my first one.

Tuesday night and I had 11 people for the dive on Sunday. The boat had been booked and we were due to dive out of Portsmouth. The skipper was not well known to me, but I had been out with him on a number of other trips organised by other people from the club and he had said due to the short notice of the trip, there was no need to send a deposit.

On the Saturday night, as advised by the skipper, I had dialled up his number just to make sure the weather was OK. This was just a formality. I knew this because the weather had been hot and sunny all week and the wind had been at a breeze. After a few rings, I had the skipper on the other end of the phone and it was not what I wanted to hear. "You what?" I challenged; he had double booked and was taking the other party because he had taken their booking before mine. Well, that was just great. "What about someone else?" I asked; did he have any other options to offer me? No, he didn't. Very sorry he was, but that was that, as far as he was concerned. Hanging up, I let him know what I thought of him and his sloppy business and that I wouldn't be recommending him to anyone I knew in the near future.

I had to try a find an alternative boat and skipper, but this was Saturday night and my chances were slim. I called a fellow diver, Steve Perry, in Exeter. He used the same skipper every week and had told me he would get you on the wreck and was reliable.

Well, I was not swamped with any other options, so I gave him a call. The phone rang just twice and was answered. "Hi,

Maurice speaking". After a quick introduction and explanation for my last minute call for a dive charter for tomorrow, to my amazement the boat was available. He had received a cancellation earlier that week. "Great! I will see you tomorrow, 7.30 am". All I now needed to do was call the other divers who still thought we were diving out of Portsmouth. There were only 2 that decided they would not be able to get to Exmouth as they were camped at Portsmouth for the night. This would be the start of many good years of diving with Maurice Webb and his boat *MV Grace*.

The boat was a steel, open back, purpose built dive boat. We loaded 20 cylinders and all our dive gear on her and set off with the sun rising to the stern. Everyone was relaxed and we were soon on the dive site. The wreck of the *Bretagne* was a well dived wreck location, although we had not dived her before. The skipper soon hooked the grapnel in to the wreck and secured the other end of the line with a large buoy. Kitting up back then did not take long as we were all in wetsuits, basic scuba gear, one cylinder, ABLJ for buoyancy, fins, mask and weight belt; that was about it.

Diving in pairs, we went over the side or off the stern in to the water. The visibility was 8 metres and although the wreck was fairly broken up, it was a pretty interesting dive. Back on the boat at lunch time, Maurice dished out hot dogs and burgers, washed down with mugs of hot tea. I had been on plenty of other hard boats, but this was by far the best for culinary refreshment and good humoured boat skippers. It was discussed and agreed that we would be using this boat for next year's diving.

As we were in late September now, there would be no further boat diving that year, but that's not to say we sat about until Easter the following year just talking about it; we were young and keen as mustard and any water would do.

There was a group of divers within the club that collected bottles and once a month, they held a meeting called the bottle club. So, where did these bottles come from? Not that far away as it turned out. Just up the road was a river system Bill Flower knew the location of and volunteered to take me and my brother out to Saltford the following week. It was now late November and the sun was not gracing us with its warmth, so we would have to improvise some sort of means to get warm after the dive. As we entered the water from the river bank the cold water invaded the warmth of my suit within minutes and it was as black as night under the water. Although I was only in 8 to 10 feet of water, on the bottom, digging in the mud, I had managed to find some bottles, all done by touch. The bottles were placed in to my goodie bag and I had forgotten all about the cold. 45 minutes had passed and I had a bag full of things. Now I really was cold; time to end the dive. At the surface, steam and exhaled breath hung in the air. The water temperature was about 4 degrees and the air temperature was not much better.

Back on the bank, we had to get out of our cold wetsuits and we were damn cold, but Bill had a secret weapon for this situation. How ingenious, a garden sprayer full of hot water with a shower head attached to the flexible clear tubing that would have been used originally to connect a spray gun to the end. After a few pumps in to the tank containing the hot water, hey presto, we had a hot shower. I showered off and whilst the hot water was doing its thing, I peeled myself out of my wetsuit. Within 5 minutes, I was warm, clean and back in my winter land clothes, ready for a visit to the Bird in Hand for a couple of pints and a cheese toasty before heading home for a well deserved, hot Sunday roast. It was just your typical Sunday.

Although it was a great way of keeping dive fit, it was fairly limited diving and one particular day whilst digging, something swam past me brushing against my face. My mind raced as to what it was: an eel? a fish? a rat? a body? "That's enough" I told myself, but as I could not see it, I soon decided I could do without this and aborted the dive. The next time I dived a river, it was thousands of miles away and an alligator was my surprise river companion, but that's another story.

The next few years were spent with a committed dive crew comprising 12 eager divers pushing the boundaries and exploring new wrecks and dive sites all around the UK's south coast. Most of these were off the dive boat *MV Grace* with her trusty skipper Maurice.

The dive crew, as we looked upon ourselves, were quite a collection of different people from different walks of life, but we were all drawn together through the common passion of diving. As the dive season wound down for winter in 1987, I sat down with the Dive Devon guide book and put plans together to dive the various wrecks that Devon had to offer.

The first dive started with a shake up dive in April 1988 on the *Empress of India* in 48 metres, with weekend trips running right through to September. After committing the dates to the skipper, all I had to do was fill the other 11 spaces and get the deposits sent out to secure the bookings. I needn't have worried; the deposits came in the very next week. If only all things in life were as easy as that.

Let me spend a few moments introducing you to the dive crew as they were there with me for many years.

Derek Cook worked in insurance and was keen to have a laugh. He was also a club instructor and was keen to dive anything that was deep, in UK waters or in the Med. We would later on in life get into some serious deep water trouble in 79 metres of water off the coast of Malta. How the hell could this happen? Very easily, if you put yourself in a reckless situation.

Bill Batey worked as a copier engineer and was an excellent club instructor. Although he was nearly twenty years older than us, he was there on most of the dives, rain or shine. I can recall one particularly funny evening when we were camping as usual, down at Ladram Bay. There were twelve of us and we were booked on the *MV Grace* for Saturday and Sunday. It was Saturday night and after spending the evening at the club house, Andy and I walked back to our tent to catch up with Bill who had left us much earlier that evening. Arriving back at the tent, we were met by Bill who had had a few more drinks than us. After a few stories from the past, the rain began to empty down on us and so we called it a night.

Andy and I were first in to the tent and were in our sleeping bags by the time Bill appeared in the door way of the ridge tent, swaying as he steadied himself on the centre pole at the entrance. All of a sudden, he fell in to the tent bringing down the pole and the rest of the tent on top of us all. Well, Andy and I were in hysterics and Bill just scrambled in to his sleeping bag, mumbled some words and then fell asleep. What sort of a mate wrecks the tent and then falls fast asleep? We laughed again. The rain kept falling and the fabric of the tent lay across us with small puddles of water now forming in the uneven parts. We could have tried to fix the tent that night, but it was late, raining and we just couldn't be bothered, so we just left it how it was. Bill was now snoring. Well, at least someone was happy. It is true that ignorance is bliss.

In the morning, Bill was up at 7 o'clock, cooking our breakfast: bacon and scallops. I thought he had missed the sad excuse for a tent, but no. "Hey Dave, what happened to the tent?" he asked as I climbed out of what was my tent. "Funny you should ask Bill. You pulled it down last night when you sort of fell on it". Needless to say, he couldn't remember a thing and we laughed about it all over again. After breakfast, he did manage to straighten the poles and it was as good as new. What a guy, selective memory, top chef, and structural engineer and all before breakfast.

Rick Ayrton, a practicing dentist, father of two and keen diver, although I have never had the pleasure of him attending to my gnashers. Friends and business should be kept separate if at all possible, especially if they are going to cause you pain. Rick would later go on to make some underwater programmes for the BBC called Deep Wreck Mysteries.

Andy Mawditt worked in office sales and gave me my first crash course in sales, shortly before I joined a sales team to further my career. I have been in sales ever since; I must remember to write him out of my will. Andy was not a lazy person by any means, but when it came to getting up in the mornings he was hopeless. We, being good mates, often ended up taking down the tent around him, leaving him in his sleeping bag in the middle of an empty field. It made little difference to his slumber, and we just had to leave him there to surface in his own good time.

Dave Gould worked for Volvo as a mechanic and was a keen caver turned diver. He was very calm and focused on whatever he was doing. He took me on my first caving trip on the Mendips and after an hour, we reached the first of two sumps. There was a shallow pool of water against a wall of rock and all I had to do was hold my breath and pull myself through. With the gravel rubbing my face and the rock ceiling on my back, I pulled myself through to where he was standing. We were now between two sumps and he asked if I wanted to continue, but at that point, I had to confess that I had had enough. We later dived a large mine in north Wales; it's better with diving apparatus.

Chris Charles worked in a dive shop that he ran for Richard Bull. In between chasing women and going diving, he later went on to own his own dive shop in Bristol.

Darren Woodward, electrician, prankster, keen deep diver and long time friend. We dived together for many years on some fantastic wrecks. He later went on to use a re-breather for all his diving with most of his dives taking him deeper than sixty metres and has turned into 'Romer Treece' from the film The Deep.

Ian Gregory was the crazy plumber who could swear for England and get you thrown off a campsite in two minutes, but he would always help you out if you were in a fix, especially if he got you in to it. However, he was serious entertainment value when it came to dive trips and diving. We were all in Scapa Flow one year and he was bunking down with Gary Trent when he threw all his smelly socks over the side. Later in his diving years, he got himself lost in the wreck of the Hood just in the breakwater at Plymouth. He did get out after an hour, but I think it shook him up quite a lot!

Jeff Horton had a young family, but his first born was such a good baby that he and his wife, who was also a diver, took him everywhere and I never saw him cry once (the baby, not Jeff!) He was the first true foodie I had ever met and he never stopped surprising me by what he was happy to eat. As I remember, he was also keen on bashing off bits of brass from the Empress of India. On one occasion I had to tap him on the shoulder inside the wreck and almost take the hammer from him before he would come out and end the dive.

Myself - I had just got married and taken up diving, changed jobs and was working for a vehicle rental business after my crash course in sales by my good friend and realist Andy Mawditt (on the way back from a caving weekend in his car). I was very fortunate in the fact that I just selected various dive locations and all my mates and their mates just signed up for them. I have always been blessed with the fact that either I was fun to be with or I just knew what I and all my friends wanted to do, either way it worked for all of us.

Although there were some that picked and chose the dives and dates they were able to come on, I never had a problem filling the boat with eager divers.

Deep wrecks and dive locations

The dive sites were plentiful and one of the ones that we all were keen to dive was the *HMS Empress of India*. 15,000 tonnes of First World War, decommissioned pre-dreadnaught battleship in 48 metres of water. It was a formidable dive for us as most of us had never been that deep before. Although we had all experienced nitrogen narcosis, it had been at much lesser depths and so its effects were proportional to that depth.

We set out from Exmouth with the sun shining in the early morning sky. Our hi-tech equipment consisted of a cylinder, a wetsuit, knife, fins, small hand held torch, demand valve and an ABLJ which resembled a toilet seat that went over your head and secured round your back and under the crotch. It could be inflated two ways: one via a direct feed from the demand valve first stage attached to the cylinder or by the emergency cylinder that was tucked in to the ABLJ and could be filled from the main dive cylinder by decanting compressed air from it before each dive.

After about 2 and a half hours we got kitted up and prepared for the dive. We all had our dive buddies and once the grapnel was secured in the wreck, we went over the side in to the flat, calm water and down the shot line. At 25 metres, I could feel the effects of nitrogen narcosis, but I felt quite able to continue. At 37 metres, I landed on what I thought was the sea bed, but unless we were in the wrong place, it should be at 48 metres. It was then we both realised we were on the hull of the upside down battleship. It was quite light and I could see 6 metres or so in front of me. At this depth, time was short and the clock was ticking, so without a moment's hesitation, I set off dropping down over the port side. As I stood on the sea bed and looked back up the port side, I could see large port holes that ran along the side. These were set about five feet up from the sea bed. All of the super structure was buried. The wreck was huge by any standards. I spent just a few minutes looking in awe and was very aware of the effects of nitrogen narcosis as I listened to the exhaust bubbles flowing from my regulator.

I checked my air and bottom time. We had been in the water 7 minutes and it was time to head back to the shot line and commence our ascent in order to avoid lengthy decompression. I pressed the inflation button on my ABLJ and listened to the air hiss in to it. I did not rise an inch for a nervous minute. I had thoughts of not being able to get off the bottom; had my ABLJ got a hole in it? Was I running out of air? I cracked the emergency bottle and to my relief felt myself become buoyant. Derek and I looked at each other and made our way back to the shot line and back up to the surface. Wow, what a dive. This was the deepest and biggest wreck we had done so far and I must say we were impressed, although deep diving with Derek would reach far greater depths in years to come, almost costing me my life.

We continued to dive the many wrecks around Devon over the next few years and year in, year out, all I had to do was book the boat and 11 people paid up and turned up without a moment's hesitation. On Tuesday nights, we met at the club, put together a plan of action, drank beer and generally had a great time. No one seemed to worry about drink driving at the time and the club was just getting bigger and bigger. Every week, new members continued to join up; some came and went soon after their training, but most of them stayed around.

Although there were plenty of club dives, I was more inclined to sign up for the hard boat dives. I can remember some eventful days of missing wrecks, broken equipment and being recovered back to shore. It's always the best intentions that seem to be the catalyst for these eventful occasions.

We once headed out in two full dive boats with a guy called Selwyn in his speed boat. We had launched from Fort Bovisand near Plymouth and the weather looked good. We all shipped out together, but on the way the speed boat developed a fuel problem and so we let him have our spare fuel tank. This would prove to be a bad mistake. He got his boat going and we set off again. We got to the dive site and dropped anchor tying the 2 dive boats together. As we glanced across to the speed boat, Selwyn was shouting.

I could see the boat was low in the water and in the time it took me to untie our boat, the only thing left out of the water was 4 feet of his bow. As I remember it, a larger boat took him in tow back to Fort Bovisand and we continued the dive. Once one boat load had completed their dive, they headed back and we finished up our dive, pulled up the anchor and headed for home. Within 10 minutes, we were out of fuel. What a situation. We bobbed about for over 3 hours until a hard boat called the *Excalibur* pulled alongside. Once we told him we were out of fuel he gave us hell and took us in tow. He then called Fort Bovisand and got them to announce we were out of fuel and being towed in. Bill Lewis was mortified at the mess we had got ourselves in to, all in the name of sport diving. What can I say? It was a sequence of events and a right bloody circus. Club boats and half thought out random actions. Well, they will always have a nasty way of biting you in the ass. This wasn't the first time and certainly wouldn't be the last.

As with all clubs, certain members were more active in organising dives. Bill Lewis was a first class BSAC diver and club instructor. On one fateful day, not long after our recent fiasco, he organised a hard boat dive out in the Solent just off the Isle of White. The dive site, as I remember, was a sub. The skipper was not someone we had used before and he had a Polish lady on board who would be crewing and cooking for us on the day.

Without further ado, we loaded our kit onboard. The boat was an off shore 105 with twin engines and a forward wheel house full of electronic gadgets. Steaming out towards the dive location, the sea got choppy and the skipper was now searching with his electronic instruments for the wreck. After about 20 minutes, the sea was getting rougher and the first shot line was sent over the side followed by another and another. The skipper was now agitated and was about to completely lose it big time. Bill was concerned about the deterioration of the weather and the ability of the skipper; so was I.

The skipper had pointed to the 4 shot lines marked with bright orange buoys and announced that the wreck was somewhere between them. It was not under any of the 4 buoys that were now marking where it wasn't. Oh dear. We had now pulled out a huge piece of steel plate as a make-shift shot line. Again, he missed the wreck and now wanted to start pulling up some of the failed buoys because there was nothing left to throw over the side. We had been going round and round for over an hour and the sea had now got an eight feet swell to it. We had now had quite enough and after a quick discussion with the rest of the divers we decided to abort this dive site and look for one with a bit more shelter, perhaps even one the skipper could locate.

Bill, as the organiser of the trip had the arduous pleasure of telling our skipper. Well, to say he was not impressed with our decision was very clear. He started shouting and charging round the boat pulling up some of the shot lines. The first two came up but the next one was stuck fast and that's when he lost it big time. Entering the wheel house, ranting and raging, he pushed both throttles to their stops, the boat leapt forward and we all hugged on to the wheel house for our lives as the boat crashed through what was now a 10 foot swell. Pitching from left to right, at this point we thought he was about to capsize the boat and a less sturdy boat would have probably sunk. After 5 minutes the skipper regained sense and reason and lowered the power and began to apologise for his outrageous behaviour, but we had our own opinion of him by now. This crazy bastard could have caused a major accident or worse.

We got to a sheltered bay just off the pleasure beach at Shanklin, Isle of White. The Polish lady appeared with what could only be described as mutton stew. The meat was like rubber and all we could salvage from it was to dip our bread in the liquid and the rubber meaty bits went over the side at discreet intervals. To our great amusement, the seagulls swooped down and ate it, only to drop chunks back in to the sea. "Bloody Hell, not even a scavenger of the sea could eat it!" Bill exclaimed.

After the morning's events, we spent 2 hours at the pleasure beach and were late getting back to the boat. The skipper was off again shouting and stomping about, so we called it a day and we headed back to port and disembarked the boat vowing never to set foot on it again. Some months later, the skipper and hard boat made print and all for the wrong reasons. Some people should never leave land let alone be in charge of a boat.

Back at the dive club a few weeks later, Bill had organised some lectures, along with some guest speakers, all part of ongoing training. At one particular navigating lecture, an elderly naval chap turned up. He had been in the navy all his life and spoke with great command and confidence on the subject of charts, tides and navigation. He had brought along some of his own charts and after a 40 minute talk, he got a few people up to the front with him to do some practical plotting on his precious charts. We knew they were precious because one guy took the compass and stuck them deep in to the paper charts and he bellowed at them with great naval authority. The poor guy was frozen by this unexpected reprimand and the whole place went silent. Bill quickly defused the moment and the lecture proceeded. Next time he asked for a volunteer the hands were very hesitant. All in all, he was a very knowledgeable man and was used to dealing with professional naval personnel not a bunch of happy go lucky sport divers. At the end, he invited questions and one girl asked some very random unintelligent questions. He responded in an appropriate manor, his patience nearly spent. However, the last question she managed was a classic. Earlier he had warned us about who you should and shouldn't go to sea with and she now asked him for an example of this situation. "Lady," he said, "I wouldn't go sailing with you, if you were the last f ing person on Earth". Bill quickly turned off the video recorder and she got the point nearly as quickly. With that scathing statement, Bill closed the lecture before things got any more personal. What a bloody laugh. These old naval sea dogs just say it as it is, they don't suffer fools, period.

After the naval man had left, we all had a good laugh and smile at it. Bill asked if we wanted to stay for an hour, to have a look at some technical diving incidents and equipment that was happening over in America. That was the first taste of things to come within the UK dive market.

Bill had some news on father and son team Chris Rouse Sr. and Chris Jr. who had lost their lives on a wreck called the *U Who*, an unknown submarine that John Chatterton and Richie Kohler had discovered. They had both suffered a rapid buoyant ascent from 230 feet missing all their stops.

Technical diving is on its way

The equipment and gas mixes Americans had available was awe inspiring and would require a whole new set of skills, knowledge and equipment in order to use them safely. I was just getting comfortable with my basic kit; it would be a few years before I was actively pushing these boundaries.

With diving all through the year, a wetsuit was not the best choice and drysuits had just started to come on to the market at an affordable price. The first one I was able to own was a second hand, laminated membrane type that you stepped in to through the shoulder zip. It had no boots, just latex ankle seals and latex wrist seals. To prevent the suit from squeezing you as you dived deeper and the water pressure increased there was an air feed from the dive cylinder to a valve on the suit. As you went deeper, the pressure increased and was equalized by putting air in to the suit to match the external pressure. Simple, but essential. Now there's only one thing worse than a cold wetsuit in October and that's a leaky drysuit and back in the day, these drysuits did not last too long before they started to leak. This suit was no exception and no sooner had I bought it and got used to it, the thing leaked like hell. There was only one option: spend some more money & get a new one.

The problem was two fold. They weren't cheap and there was not a lot of choice. After convincing my wife Kay, that a new suit was a must and that it would last many years, I decided to opt for a suit made of neoprene, the same material as a wetsuit but with water tight stitching boots sewn in and neck and wrist seals. It was made to measure and the company was in Somerset if any repairs were needed at a later point. DMS measured up and posted the suit out to me 3 weeks later. All that was left to do was get diving.

The first dive was on the *Empress of India*, 48 metres. Wow, what a difference! Dry, warm and 15 minutes deco. I could now dive all year round in relative comfort. There were a few down sides, well just one: you couldn't just have a pee when you wanted one. Apart from that, it was all good.

Scapa Flow

In 1990, with the start of a new diving season, I had booked the first of many trips to Scapa Flow. It was booked for May and there were a mixed bunch of us, half in drysuits and the rest in wetsuits. This would sort the men from the boys, as they say.

I had hired a 17 seat mini bus as it was the cheapest way to get to Orkney. I just hadn't realised how long it was going to take to get there at 65 mph. I had arranged to meet everyone at key meeting points. Space would be the biggest issue with 12 divers with sleeping bags and dive kit in a 17 seat bus and no roof rack. Driving round to John and Julie's, it was clear we wouldn't all get in, so John offered to take his car. We set off sharing the driving as we went. 14 hours later we got to Scrabster in the early hours. It was one of the most desolate and barren places I had seen. There was nothing open and we had no B&B booked, so it was going to be a long, cold, uncomfortable night all spent in a mini bus.

Thank Goodness, Derek had brought a case of Newquay Steam beer. At 6.5 % we were all soon in a semi coma, snoring and farting! Day break was a pleasant relief, as you can imagine. We found a café and after bacon butties and gallons of tea we were semi human again and there was just the ferry to board.

Onboard the P&O ferry we settled down, and enjoyed the crossing, with its stunning wild landscape, before arriving in Stromness at 2 o'clock. Once the ferry had docked, we walked down the gangway and found the boat. She was called *Sunrise*. The skipper met us at her mooring, I did the pleasantries and we were welcomed aboard.

Sunrise was a converted 70 feet fishing trawler, with a purpose built covered bow so us tough divers could keep warm and dry whilst getting changed and waiting to get in the water. How great was that? By the time all the kit was on the boat and I had nabbed my bunk, it was late afternoon and Mark, the skipper, got us together for a brief on the dos and don'ts of the boat.

Mark and his wife Debbie had been operating the boat for a few seasons and were well used to us divers, whilst being laid back and great hosts; they must have had the patience of saints.

The boat had fresh water tanks, 2 sea flush toilets, galley, 6 double bunks, central heating, main saloon room, compressor, and 2 fresh water showers.

Debbie would be cooking breakfast for us, served after our first dive. What more could we ask for? It was Saturday evening and the pub beckoned us for some local beers. 80 Shillings was the choice of the masses.

The Ferry Inn was used by divers and the locals kept themselves to themselves. That's OK; beer is a good leveller for all men, women and divers. After a few beers, happy and tired, it was back to the boat for supper and a good night's sleep.

Although my bunk was very warm and comfortable I had not taken in to account the other 11 people all taking it in turns snoring and farting all night long. Sleep would be a luxury. I resolved to drink more the next night.

I was sharing a bunk with Derek and he was the last to get up, not just one day, but every day. Debbie encouraged this by saving him toast and orange juice. I fear she thought we may eat the lot and leave him zilch. What was she thinking? He's a good mate amongst mates; damn right we would, just for the Hell of it - that's what mates do.

We chugged out of port and headed for the first dive site.

We were doing 3 dives per day and my trusty suit was leaking. Every morning, I pulled myself in to it and it was getting wetter and more uncomfortable every time I put it on. Nevertheless, I was better off than the poor people in wetsuits. With a water temperature of 6 degrees, the wetsuiters had resorted to heading for the shower rooms in their wetsuits after every dive, turning on the showers and slowly getting out of their suits whilst warming up. Damned ingenious, but just one small problem: Mark, the skipper got us all together and reminded us we were not plumbed in to the mains and there were only fresh water refills for the 2 tanks at port. In 2 years of running the boat, we were the most wasteful bunch he had ever had on the boat. So, that was that, we had been told. On that note, they promised to be quicker and it seemed to work.

As the week progressed the nights got later and later. One thing to remember was the Skipper and his wife lived on the boat at the stern next to the galley. In hindsight, not the best place when there are 12 hungry, boozy divers on form, fresh from the pub.

They were as good as gold. They didn't complain too much, even when we changed the dive start time from 7 am to 8 and then to 8.30. Yes, it got later each day; something to do with the pace of the week, diving, drinking and late nights. It tended to take its toll.

Derek, being Derek, had given us all nick names. I was "Damp suit Blackmore", Derek was "Dangerous Derek", John and Julie "Blue lips Duckett" as they were now the only two wetsuit divers left, Mike "Money bag" Haigh, "Mine's a double single malt" Batey and Jeff "I don't mind driving" Gully.

That night we were planning to meet up with 4 other boats at a small island pub for a meal and get together. The pub was packed and the drinks were flowing. Mark and his mate Keith had filled a Viking hat with spirits & some of the guys had a wee sip but I gave it a miss. I didn't know what was in it, but it smelled like Vicks sinex.

Mark's mate Keith would later prove to be a big influence on the dive I would carry out on the *HMS Hampshire*, but for now, I needed my bunk if I was to stand any chance of diving tomorrow.

The week's diving was just getting better. For the third dive of the day, we were diving Gutter Sound. This was where 67 ships of the interned German fleet had remained at anchor for many months before they were sent to the bottom during a simultaneous scuttling in June 1919.

Derek and I were diving with the tidal flow and covering a lot of ground as we drifted. Three feet off the sea bed, Derek spotted a shell case a metre long and we quickly wrestled it in to a goodie bag. Back on board the *Sunrise* we all had trinkets and souvenir bottles, china cups, plates and jars, but the shell case was the first prize, later to sit on the bar at the dive club. By then, it had all our names on it and Bill had put a false top on it so we could use it to drop our loose change in to.

Although I had seen many shell cases over the years their sheer size and potential never escapes me and on one sunny afternoon we brought up 24 3 foot shells from a wreck called the *America*. Once the heads had been hit off with a hammer and all the cordite was despatched in to the sea we were allowed back aboard the dive boat; what a find! All that was left to do was the removal of the 4 inch detonators firmly fixed in the base of the shell; they unfortunately looked like new, ready to go bang at the slightest provocation. Expert knowledge was needed as I had all 24 of them now sat in my garage & my wife Kay was none too pleased! These things had now stared to dry out and would make random noises from time to time as you walked past them.

I had met a man earlier in the year who said he had been an explosives guy in the forces, who lived in Trowbridge. I can't remember his name but I did remember him volunteering to defuse any bombs I found. Oh really! I called him up and he said pop round – fantastic! I loaded all 24 shells in to my car and off I went; I parked up in the cul-de-sac and rang his door. 'Hi, how you doing?' Very well thanks.' With the pleasantries over we got down to the job in hand; he came over to the car and took a look. "Oh! there's a lot," he exclaimed! I could tell he was not at ease with the situation. He took a look and began to explain how the detonator could be removed without it exploding. Well F**k, that's what I thought you were there for! The next thing his partner came out and went ballistic. He was very uneasy and asked me to leave (to preserve his relationship), so I did just that. When I got home Kay was pleased to see me until I told her that the guy hadn't disarmed the dam things, and at that point she made it clear - get rid of them, or else!

At the time I was working for Gulliver's Truck Rental and one of the fitters had expressed a keen interest in getting his hands on them so without further ado, one night at 6.30 he took a cold chisel to the base of the shells and hit all 24 detonators out of them!! I was scared when he did the first two, but it all seemed fine after that. I held them in my hand and they looked like new and could have taken your fingers off if they had gone bang! Lucky we can still play the fiddle!!

Back on the *Sunrise* it was Thursday and Keith, the skipper of another dive boat, had 2 American divers that wished to join us for a dive on the battleship *Kron Prince Wilhelm*. 25,000 tonnes and upside down in 38 metres of water, we had a quick discussion and agreed they could join us. We dropped down the anchor line and landed on what looked like the sea bed at about 25 metres. It was, in fact, the hull of this mighty ship. The visibility was 10 metres as we swam down over the hull to look for something of interest. There it was, a brass port hole looking like it would just fall off in to our hands with a little bit of gentle persuasion. After 5 minutes working on it, I decided it may need a lot more brute force than we had bargained for. Dropping to the sea bed, I found a 4 ft bar and brought it up to use on the port hole, but it still refused to move and with all the extra exertion, I was low on air and had to leave it. We would have to try and locate it tomorrow, our last day.

That night we planned, gathered our tools and worked out a plan to finish what we had started. I briefed Mark, the skipper, on our plans for the morning dive over a few beers. He seemed OK with it.

That night Jeff Horton began eating some horse mussels. After a quick glance, I reassured him he could have the lot. I was happy with a 12 oz steak from the Ferry Inn. I hit my bunk and slipped quickly in to a deep sleep; all the late nights and early starts were beginning to take their toll, not to mention the three dives a day.

To my surprise, we were all up at 8 am and the first dive team was in the water by 8.45 am. After 5 minutes, the tools were sent down the shot line. To say it all went smoothly would be a lie; the first team failed to find the port hole, the bag opened and most of the tools were lost, and to top it all you couldn't see more than 3 metres. It was the worst visibility we had seen all week. Needless to say, that old port hole got to stay.

Whilst we were all faffing about, Bill was spotted low on air. Derek offered him his spare reg, but he just signalled back to him that he would breathe off his ABLJ. Crikey, this man had balls! I am buggered if I would want to breathe off an ABLJ at 38 metres. There must be something in the whisky!

We all had our stories of why we failed to retrieve the port hole. However, the main reason was due to the fact that as the American divers had been with us when we had to leave it the day before, we had not tied a line and marked its location in case they got back first and claimed it. What were we thinking of? Greed and mistrust over some old bit of brass, whatever next?

To understand this behaviour, it's necessary to get a feel for the average diver. There are 2 types of divers: one likes to look at fish, take photos and generally admire the wonder of the sea. This normally takes them to exotic warm places abroad or on shallow reefs and bays around the UK. Then there's the other type, the wreck diver. These people are committed to visiting wrecks that have history, providence and intrigue. If I had to sum it up, it would be similar to climbers and mountains; if you ask a climber why they climb certain mountains, they would say "because it's there" and it's the same for wreck divers.

Everest's of the deep like *Lusitania, Britannic, Andrea Doria, Hampshire* and the pride of the German fleet, lying at the bottom of Scapa Flow. Yes, we wanted to dive them, touch them, but a trophy like a port hole would be a coup and would stand pride of place in memory of the week spent diving these great ships. Don't get me wrong, I do respect these old wrecks and the war grave issue, but most of these wrecks have been dived, touched and had artefacts removed from them long before I had the opportunity to dive them. As far as I am concerned, it's all about who is diving, what's at stake and who will make something out of it. The wreck of the *Edinburgh*, loaded with gold, though sunk with a huge loss of life and certainly a war grave, was salvaged with the blessing of the British government. What's the difference?

By the end of the week, we were all a bit tired and cold after logging 18 dives each. After packing all our dive kit into a crate, we relaxed on the deck. Jeff Horton was eating again and although it looked edible, who could tell what he had been eating prior to this? Something that would later have its revenge, let me tell you.

Saturday morning we said our goodbyes and boarded the ferry. All we wanted to do was get on the road and home. It would be a long day with 700 miles to cover and took nearly 14 hours driving.

After a short stint at the wheel, Jeff Gully was relieved of his driving stint after the rear wheels to the mini bus bounced off another random rock at the edge of a 40 foot drop at the side of what was laughingly called the road.

We each took our turn at the wheel and after 2 hours Jeff Horton did not look too well. He suffered in relative silence for a few more hours, but by now he looked ghastly. We got him drinking water and shortly after, we noticed a grey/blue discolouring to his face. "That's not good" we thought and as we got within 100 miles of Glasgow, we asked Jeff whether he felt well enough to carry on or did he want to be taken to hospital. If he was admitted, we would need to carry on, so he was adamant he would hang in there and carry on. Like a true trooper he did, with the grey pallor travelling around his body.

Arriving at Bristol, Jeff was looking better and we knocked on his door first. It was 2 am and his wife greeted us. She looked concerned seeing Jeff, but after we told her how bad he had been and that he now looked 50% better, she seemed a bit more at ease. He made a full recovery and was grateful we did not leave him at Glasgow. I can tell you it was a close call as he was very ill at the time.

Over the next 2 years, I continued to dive mainly with the club and enjoyed a great social side whenever we met up on a Tuesday night or away on a dive. As with most clubs, they have their highs and lows and at the time, it was on a high; some keen new guys had joined the club, eager to engage in some more challenging diving.

Quick actions to save a life

In 1993 with new found diving friends the next Scapa trip was organised. Half the divers were from Dave and Sandra Gould's club and although I didn't know them all, they were a good bunch.

We went in 2 transit vans. Darren was in the white van, and Ian Gregory in his Green one. Meeting up at Dave Gould's house on Friday 31st May 1993, the sun was shining and every one was keen to get moving. Some of us had been before and knew it would be a long trip. The plan was to take it in turns to drive. Darren did the first stint and I did the second. We got up to the Scottish border and Dave Gould drove like a bat out of Hell, up through the Highlands. He was used to driving 38 tonne vehicles and had no trouble slinging the Transit round the bends. We were listening to Jethro at the time, which was a first for me and it appealed to my sense of humour, taking my mind off the white knuckle ride in the passenger seat of the van.

Needless to say, we arrived in good time to get in to the pub at Kirkwall. Not a lot had changed here, still as run down as ever. Although there were a lot of us in the pub, you still felt like an outsider and the bar staff made sure you knew it. They served us last every time a local was waiting, but we didn't make a fuss; we were on holiday and the locals out numbered us 3 to 1.

I teamed up with Darren Woodward for the week's diving. We had dived together prior to this trip and got on well on land and in the water.

The rest of the group were a pretty mixed bag, all characters in their own right. Ian Gregory and Gary Trent took the mickey out of each other all week; it was entertainment, as Darren would say, and who could argue with that? To set the scene, you would need to know a little bit about Ian.

I first met Ian when he joined Number Three Club in the early 90s. Along with Darren, he was a great laugh and would take the mickey out of anyone who deserved it. Friend or stranger, it made no difference, he would just open his mouth and out it would come, along with plenty of strong language. Some people were offended, but that didn't make a scrap of difference. Having said that, he was just as happy to have the mick taken out of himself, so fair was fair.

As I recall Darren, Ian and I were diving out of Weymouth one summer and we had arranged to meet up on some family campsite. We had been out diving all day and each of us had a huge bag of scallops. Pulling on to the site in the tatty green Transit van of Ian's, the owner of the site approached us and said "no all male parties" to Ian. Before we could say we were with a mixed group already camped on the site, Ian had called him all the names and mothers under the sun and was wheel spinning on the grass as we exited the site. "What did you do that for Ian?" I asked, "Well, he can stick his poxy campsite, we will find somewhere else". OK, off we went, but failed to find one that would take three men in a tatty Transit. We parked up and found a pub. Getting to the bar, Darren asked to see the head chef or manager. Out came the manager, "do you want to buy some scallops?" At that point, we produced three bags of scallops. "Bloody Hell, what do you want for them?" he said. After 5 minutes of haggling, we settled on half a dozen beers each and a pub meal of any choice from the menu. The van was now parked on a building site and that was to be our camp site for the night. After a few pints of Stella, it did'nt matter a damn where we slept. Nice one Ian.

As I touched on earlier, the divers on this trip were made up from 2 clubs. I knew most of them, but you can never tell when a sequence of events will open up a life and death situation and who will be involved.

The sea state and visibility underwater was some of the best you could wish for and all the dives up until then went without a hitch. We were all diving with long term buddies and had many dives logged. It was mid week and we were diving one of the light cruisers at a depth of 34 metres. Due to the depth and dive plan, most dive pairs planned to carry out some decompression stops.

Darren and I were planning on a maximum dive time and would spend 15 to 20 minutes decompressing at the end of the dive. Whilst we were happily carrying out our deco stops, things were about to take a turn for the worst for one pair.

A young husband and wife team Garry and Mary came up the shot line where Dave and Sandra were carrying out there deco stops. Just before they reached Dave and Sandra, Marie lost her fin and made a grab for it. In doing so she let go of the shot line. The fin swiftly disappeared in to the dark depths and so did she. Her husband Garry just froze; who knows what was racing through his mind. Dave was expecting him to go after her, but that was not about to happen. These things life and death situations come about so quickly and people either freeze at that point or go in to auto mode ignoring all rational thoughts and common self preservation. At that point Dave took direct action. Ignoring the fact that he should finish his decompression, and all the warning bells ringing in his head, he chased down in to the blackness hoping against all odds that he could locate her because by now she was nowhere to be seen. These situations can make you feel sick with the thoughts of what you could find or have to face back on the surface if it all goes horribly wrong and lets face it things were not looking good. Her husband Garry looked on in desperation. Some people do say that it's not always a good idea to pursue extreme sports as a couple or kin just because sometimes you could find yourself in a situation where you may have to make a choice between your son, wife or partner and yourself. Who can say? What a horrid place to be, and in these situations both people could lose their lives. Dave reached the bottom at 34 metres and found her just lying on the sea bed. It was dark and he was fortunate she had not drifted far from the shot line; she was alone and the sea was about to embrace her for ever. She had one finger pressing her suit inflation valve but she wasn't going anywhere. Her other arm was raised and all the air was just purging out of her dump valve. It would just be a short matter of time before her air ran out.

Dave acted fast with a quick assessment of the situation - he took her by the arm and pulled her to her knees so that her arms fell to her sides. This achieved a number of positive things; she was now aware of her situation and that she was not alone, her finger came off the inflation valve and with some reassurance from Dave they were on their way from the sea bed. They were lucky they were not far from the shot line and this enabled them to ascend the line in a fully controlled ascent. At the surface they were both recovered to the safety of the boat and put on pure oxygen as a precaution. At this point, Darren and I finished our deco and climbed back on board where the mood was somewhat sombre.

After a few hours it was clear that Dave and the girl had not suffered any ill effects, but due to the seriousness of the incident, Dave had to miss the next day's diving. As for the husband and wife, they spent 3 days soul searching in their bunk. I think he felt that he should have been the one to save her. It's a hard one to deal with, but one thing is for sure, if Dave had not gone down and brought her up, she would have died. We can't be all things at all times, but her life was saved on the day and that was the most important thing at that moment. The pair finished their soul searching and enjoyed the rest of the week, but never dived again.

Never stop a volunteer!

As with most things that happen in life, even in the short space of just one week emotions can swing from one extreme to another & help can also come in a mixed variety. Just as Dave had come to the rescue one of our dive crew, someone else had taken it upon himself to be watchful over the ropes that tethered our boat *Sunrise* to the quay. Just to put you in the picture, our skipper Mark, a very experienced man of the sea, had from time to time asked one or two of us to help with the ropes when we came in to port. We were all happy to do this, but once done we left them alone. As you can imagine, as the sea rises and falls with the tides the boat will do the same, but only provided there is enough slack in the ropes to allow it. Steve had assisted on a few occasions and felt the need to tidy up these ropes – well, they were all loose and untidy. He soon sorted that out and took up all the slack in them - there, nice & tidy! As the tide fell the 65 tone boat *Sunrise* began to be suspended by these ropes, and it wasn't what a boat should have to deal with. I can't truly remember Mark our trusty skipper ever being so displeased with one of my trusty dive crew but lessons were learnt and limits were realised - Mark had reached his, and Steve had learnt a valuable lesson about ropes and boats! He was a bit sheepish the next day but we acknowledged him in full with a new nickname - The Rope Man of Scapa Flow. One man's help is another man's nightmare, and I am a firm believer in the saying never stop a volunteer, but some things are better sorted yourself - especially things that matter.

On the Friday night, it was decided that we all deserved a barbecue and Alex volunteered to cook it. We needed 2 separate throw away ones because there were a few vegetarians in the group. With this in mind, the girls went off to pick up the provisions. Meat, meat and more meat, onions, rolls and of course, Linda McCartney sausages and burgers. In typical fashion and tradition, the weather closed in and down came the rain, so most of us stayed in the dry on the boat. Alex battled on outside, cooking up a feast. Even the vegetarians complimented him on the food with words to the effect that these veggie burgers were the best they had ever had. Unfortunately, Alex omitted to tell them that one of the barbecues would not light and so all the food was cooked together and not truly veggie. It just goes to show you can't taste the difference. Linda McCartney would have turned in her grave and I don't think the vegetarians would be too pleased either.

Dave resumed diving after his day of rest, with no ill effects and his rescue was quite the talk of the town for a few weeks after, although no one who knew him was surprised at his quick, calm actions. I had first met Dave through a good friend at the dive club, Andy Mawditt, who had known Dave through the caving club and had invited me to come along and have a go at caving up in the Mendips. He was a wealth of knowledge and was always out and about either climbing or caving.

The Silica Mine

In the Miners Arms pub after some caving one evening, we got chatting about diving and he was keen to get involved, seeing it as an extension to his caving. It wasn't long before I was planning to join him on a dive over in north Wales; all I knew was that it was a mine.

The weekend was planned with Derek Cook, Dr John, Dave and I. Dr John and Dave were both part of the same caving club and yes, he was a proper doctor. He managed to do an op on Dave's knee in a lunch hour; it cost him a bottle of whisky. Oh, the good old days when common sense was still a part of our everyday lives and guide lines were left for individuals to make grown up decisions about. I drove all 4 of us to the dive site in my Cortina estate because I had the biggest car. Back in 1991 we were pretty much diving on basic equipment which was just as well, or we would never have got it all in the car.

Arriving at the site, we were surrounded by some large mountains. I was hoping against all the odds that the entrance would be on our level and that a climb up one of the sides of the mountains would not be necessary. However, as with most things, if it's worth doing, it's going to take some effort, and it did.

Once in our drysuits, we put our tanks on our backs together with weight belts and other dive accessories and began the climb. Once at the top, we walked for about half a mile across a field and then scrambled down some rocks to a large gaping hole cut in to the rock. I make it sound like a bit of a walk in the park, but it was far from that. I wouldn't want to give you the impression that we were unfit, so I left out the hour it took to cover the ball breaking walk to the entrance. We sat at the entrance catching our breath for 10 minutes before making our way in. The floor was covered in broken rocks, bricks and steel rods coming down from the roof. After walking for three minutes, it was pitch black and we had to use our torches just to see our hands in front of our faces. Avoiding the bars protruding from the roof and the loose rock under foot, it had taken the best part of one and a half hours to walk to this point and I did not want to twist an ankle or head butt a bar before the dive.

After 15 minutes, we stood at the water's edge. With the torches switched off, it was black as night and you could touch your face without seeing your hand at all. Dave and John went in one direction, Derek and I in another.

The water was cold and clear as gin. With a reel and line attached to the entry point, we slipped in to the water and finned slowly along the tunnel keeping to the left side. The rock had been cut out and the hole that was left was large enough to fit a truck in it, but there was only one way in and one way out. Any mistakes, like getting lost, would be paid for with our lives so we took great care as we finned on ahead not to stir up the silt and not to get tangled in the line we were laying down from the reel. After 20 minutes, we turned round and made our way back out. Following the line back, the sediment we had stirred up was held suspended in large grey clouds and was as dense as thick smoke. If you lost your line and became disorientated you would be doomed and shortly after, most probably dead. After 40 minutes, we were back at the entry point. Although there was not a lot to see, it was a good test of mental discipline in a challenging situation. There were no panic attacks and we all felt good to have done it.

It was one of those dives that having done it, you wouldn't necessarily plan to do it again. Something to do with the long hike just to get there and the thought that what if after lugging yourself and your kit all that way up there, you found that some other divers were all ready there. The silt they would stir up could take days to settle. It would be a few years before I was back there.

Technical diving has arrived in Bristol

In the early 90s, Richard Bull and his dive shop, Current State Diving, was at the fore front of technical diving and new equipment. There seemed to be something new every other month. Richard Bull would later get the prestigious job of safety diver working for the BBC, but for the time being, I knew him as the guy who owned the business. He would advise and recommend new technical training and dive equipment to suit the individual diver, so that they could carry out more challenging dives on wrecks that were now within the reach of recreational divers.

With the event of the two World Wars, there would be no shortage of classic ships to dive on. The only barriers would be their depths and locations. In order to get a better basic understanding of the limitations of what was achievable and what wasn't, it was essential for me to know my limitations and the limits of the gases I was going to use. Enter Rich Bull.

All divers start by breathing compressed air, which is fine for depths of up to 40 metres, but there is a down side to just using compressed air: nitrogen narcosis and the decompression penalties that have to be paid in time spent at different depths, allowing the nitrogen to safely come out of saturation within your body. This process is all down to the physics of gasses under pressure and how the body is affected by it.

The simple way of understanding the physics and effects of this are that the deeper and longer you spend at depth, the greater the amount of nitrogen built up as it is absorbed in to the body's tissues. To avoid getting the bends, the nitrogen must be allowed to come out of solution, slowly, through normal breathing, so that nitrogen bubbles don't form in the blood and cause a blockage, resulting in pain, paralysis or even death.

If a diver misses these stops and then gets a bend, there is only one source of treatment for them and that is to be taken to a recompression chamber where they can be safely put back under pressure. The pressure can then be gradually reduced, so the nitrogen does not form bubbles. The severity of the bend can vary from diver to diver. Some bends can be slight and leave no permanent damage at all; other bends can be crippling or even cause death.

Early in my dive training, I understood the dangers of this condition, from months of intensive lectures by knowledgeable instructors. Bill Lewis once demonstrated the effects in a simplistic, but very effective demonstration with nothing more than a bottle of lemonade. Yes, just lemonade. The gas that made it fizz represented the nitrogen and when the top was unscrewed quickly, the liquid bubbled over. If, however, it was unscrewed slowly, the bubbles were controlled and the liquid did not bubble over. This represented gas in solution and what happens when the pressure is released too quickly, the same as coming to the surface too quickly; it's as simple as that.

There is no hard and fast rule on who gets bent. Even following a strict, safe, dive plan to proven dive tables that have been tried and tested, you can still get bent. Some years later I would join the list of divers that have followed all the rules but still end up with a problem.

The technical dive scene was evolving in the USA and Richard Bull and a few others were getting involved in it so they could pass on these techniques and training skills to divers like me who wanted to dive deeper, stay longer, and dive safer. The key to this was the use of different gas mixes that we could breathe safely.

The first of these to become my choice of gas was Nitrox. Like most things, they evolve out of necessity. Over in the US, wrecks were being located in deep water and although divers were successfully diving to 70 metres just using normal air, the decompression penalties and narcotic effects were huge. They needed a gas mix that would flush out the nitrogen and enhance the mental quality of these deep dives, quicker and better than just compressed air.

Nitrox was air that had the nitrogen removed and replaced with oxygen. In order to achieve this, the cylinder is filled from empty with pure oxygen to a set pressure and then topped off with compressed air to a determined pressure.

The most popular mixes were 50% oxygen and 80% oxygen and were used specifically for decompression at pre-determined depths. Although they were a great breakthrough in speeding up the decompression process, they had a depth restriction which could cause oxygen toxicity, resulting in a black out followed by drowning if not used at the correct depths. Not a good way to end a dive. Enter Richard Bull and his new technical diver training.

My regular dive buddy, Darren, was already using this mix for deco on some deeper wrecks and its benefits were clear to see. I signed up and did the course.

I had not been in a class room for years and although I had been diving for over 10 years, it was like starting all over again with a whole new set of different rules and equipment. One thing you quickly learn in diving, nothing comes cheap, and with this new way of diving, new dive kit would be required. A man must have a hobby to spend his money on and you could certainly do this with technical diving!

After a few months, I had passed my theory and was training for the practical. This took place at Brixham. The only problem was I was booked on a dive out of Weymouth in the morning. As I recall, it was on a dive boat ferrying divers out to the wreck of the Aonian Sky. The visibility was poor and not that pleasant a dive. Back at the quay, I quickly packed up my dive kit and headed for Brixham where Rich Bull had 20 students he had been training that day. He told me he had been in and out of the water 20 times that day, so if I could kit up ASAP then we would get on with the test and he could finally go home. Well, you can't argue with that.

With a 15 litre air cylinder and 7 litre Nitrox cylinder, I swam out with Rich and we dropped down to 10 metres. The visibility was about as good as on the wreck earlier that day and we could just about see each other at a distance of four feet. The tasks went well and the hardest part was just keeping in visible contact with each other. Back on the beach I was told that I had passed; job done as far as I was concerned. The world was now my lobster as they say. There would now be dozens of quality wrecks that I could dive, that had not been possible before.

Skippers mates and free lunches

It was late summer in '93 and most of the dives were now conducted from hard boats, mainly because of the amount of technical equipment we all seemed to be using. These were the boats of choice for dive sites around Devon. We used the *MV Grace* with skipper Maurice Webb. There was no shortage of people to fill the boats maximum capacity of 12 divers. It also kept the cost down, but it was cramped on the deck; it was a catch 22, but we worked with it.

I had arranged to dive Saturday and Sunday, camping in the skipper's garden that was the size of a field. The sun was out and it was looking like a perfect weekend, weather wise.

Once we were sorted and all the tents were up, we broke out a few beers and lit up the barbecue. Maurice came round with a load of burgers and other good things to eat. We shared a few beers with him whilst the food was cooking and briefed him on our dive plans for the weekend.

We would be off early in the morning because we wanted to get 2 dives on the *Empress of India*. In order to achieve this, we had to be on the dive site for 9 am to catch the first slack water.

Down at the boat we loaded 30 cylinders and all the other dive kit aboard. There was not much space left and it was going to take a bit of organising when we all kitted up for the dive. We had all dived together loads of times before so I didn't think we would have too much trouble.

Heading out in to the sun, the sea was like glass and the air was already warming. After an hour or so, I wrote down the dive pairs on a slate. The first 4 pairs would get kitted up and then 10 minutes later the remaining 4 divers would be ready to go. Twenty minutes before we were due to reach the dive location, the first 8 started kitting up. Maurice had brought along a mate of his to help out with crewing the boat and with any assistance that the divers may have needed kitting up. It made good sense and with someone assisting, the divers could get kitted up much quicker. For all his help, Ian just wanted to have a dive, but he would have to wait until we were all in the water. He was not bothered, though he had got his eye on a port hole he had seen on the wreck a few weeks ago but was unable to lift. He had certainly come prepared this time though: 4 lifting bags, crow bars and a large hammer. I expected him to get cutting gear out at any moment or perhaps even explosives.

Right on the money, we arrived on location and the grapnel was hooked in on the wreck. I was one of the second pair in to the water and the visibility was about 10 metres at least. After a gentle journey down the shot line, I reached the upside down hull of the wreck. After swimming just a few metres I found a large hole that had been cut or blasted in to the hull. Over the years, this wreck had been salvaged for its non ferrous metals by various salvage companies. Swimming in to the hole, there were some huge pieces of machinery. I could have spent my whole dive just exploring voids in this big old wreck but we were always working against time.

I signalled to my dive buddy and we headed back to the shot line. With the visibility so good, we had no trouble finding it. This was not always the case, but for today conditions were ideal. After 15 minutes of deco stops we were back on board enjoying a cup of tea and the warmth of the morning sun. As the other divers surfaced and got back to the boat, it was clear they had all had a good dive with no incidents yet.

Ian was the only diver left in the water. That's because he was last in and he had a date with a port hole. After 10 minutes, 3 lift bags broke the surface and the skipper manoeuvred the boat in close where he could hook the bags and get whatever was attached to them. Maurice hooked the lift bags and drew them round to the stern platform of the boat. We all peered over the side to get a closer look and lend a helping hand to bring it on board. It was a port hole all right, but it was attached to a metre and a half piece of plate that must have weighed about 4 hundred weight. The port hole was close on 24 inches in diameter and it took 5 of us just to roll it on to the platform.

Ian was now on the surface. Swimming to the boat he was very excited, shouting to Maurice about the port hole. Back on board, Ian was trying to hammer the plate off the brass port hole. It was clear to all bar Ian it was not going to come off without a big ass grinder. He kept at it, but to his detriment one minute he was standing bare foot on the platform, the next minute the boat rolled slightly and the port hole and plate pinched his foot badly, cutting 4 of his toes. There was blood everywhere and Ian was hopping around the deck. Maurice was shouting to him to get his foot off the deck and stop covering it in blood. After 5 minutes, calm was restored and we had stopped the bleeding. Stitches would be required, but for now pain killers and bandages would have to do. Ian spent the rest of the day in the bunk nursing his injuries. He had stopped shouting and all the excitement in him had evaporated, poor man.

We spent the next 3 hours eating and swimming around the boat. The second dive was just as good as the first, although we had to make do without Ian's assistance as he was unable to dive. What did he care? He had his port hole and all his toes, more by luck than judgement. If it had rolled just a bit further, it would have sliced them clean off.

Back at the campsite, Maurice's field, we cooked up some more of the food Maurice had given us. Later we met up with Maurice at his local pub and the landlord greeted us with anticipation. "Do you want to eat in the bar or restaurant?", "Oh, no thanks" I reply, "We had a barbecue at Maurice's. He gave us a load of meat to cook. It was very nice: burgers, chops...", "well that's just bloody great" the landlord spouts, "I gave him that meat because it was left over from a barbecue we had!" That's when you know you have put your foot well and truly in it.

You could see the man's point, but it was too late now. Maurice didn't stick around long that night and we did our best to make up for the lack of food sales by drinking lots of beer. We all thought that it was hilarious. I bet Maurice never got free leftovers again!! We certainly didn't.!

On the Sunday morning, we met Maurice at the boat and asked him if he had any food for us. He laughed his head off and did admit he should have told us not to mention the food at the pub. Well, after that, all was fine, although he thought it would cost him dearly the next time he was in the pub.

DIY underwater Torches

As I progressed my diving through the early '90s, the wrecks got deeper and the dive kit grew. Unfortunately, back in the day, it all came at a considerable cost, whether it was a lift bag or a torch, so when my dive buddy Darren made his own 50 watt torches at a fraction of the cost of named manufactured ones, it was of great interest to me. The first prototype was only semi successful; it demanded constant dismantling in order to charge up the batteries after each dive and flooding was always a problem if meticulous attention was not taken when reassembling the battery box. A new design was needed and Darren had one.

We would use plastic soil pipe with a blank attached at each end. The batteries we would use were 3, 12 volt sealed alarm batteries, wired up 3 in a row. At one end, an RS water- tight gland was screwed in and sealed. All we needed now was some water proof lamps to house the 50 watt spot lights, originally used in kitchens and in shops for displays.

I had an old Toshiba torch that would be OK to adapt. After I drilled a hole in the base of it and fitted the RS gland, as in the battery box, I ran the wire up through the inside of the body of the torch, attaching both wires to the spot lamp. I utilised the original switch in the torch and it was sorted. The whole thing cost no more than £50, saving hundreds of pounds on a tested shop bought one. Yes, tested; that's the big unknown, but with a saving like this, it was worth the gamble, or so I thought. One day it would fail, but I would deal with that when it happened and fail it eventually did.

With these homemade 50 watt lights, I was keen to give them a try. Now it's all well and good taking them to the swimming pool to check for leaks, but the real test would be at depth, in open water. The safest option was a quarry and Stony Cove was the only deep quarry available to do this back then. The only issue was that it was in Leicestershire, miles away, but it had to be done, even though it meant leaving Bristol at about 4 am just to get a parking space in the bottom car park. My wife Kay thought I must be mad, but that's diving; It usually involves getting up at some ridiculous hour and driving hundreds of miles, but if that's what it takes, then that's what you do.

After taking them down to 34 metres with no problems, I figured they would do until they packed up or I could afford a professional one.

Fighting for life at 79 meters

As with many extreme sports, there is a gradual progression to push yourself to the limit. The problem is, you just don't know where that limit might be until you reach it. Then, when it comes, it can take you by complete surprise and throw all sorts of problems at you. If you can't evaluate the situation and sort it, then you will find yourself very much screwed or even dead.

Most major life and death situations in diving start with what might be a small problem which then rapidly spirals in to an irreversible sequence of events. It's true to say that shit happens, but all too often, the person has already started that first sequence of events before they have even got underwater.

Back in 1994, my family and I booked a holiday in Malta. We had not been there before, but our friends we were going with had. The plan was to take our basic dive kit with us and just hire the weights and cylinders. I was used to diving to 50 metres in the cold dark waters of the UK and was not fazed by diving deeper than 50 metres in these warm, clear waters. My dive buddies had dived to 60 metres last time they were over here on a diving holiday.

The flight was from Bristol Airport and just as soon as we had checked in, we were told that there was a 4 hour delay. Just the kind of thing you dread, all we could do was kick our heels and make the best of it; we were on holiday after all. By the time we boarded, we were all relaxed and the flight passed fairly quickly. Smoking and sampling our duty free; oh yes, the good old days of relaxed flying, when you could visit the flight deck and chat to the pilot if you wanted to and smoke and drink to your hearts content.

After landing in Malta and a short transfer to our accommodation, we hit the sack at about 3 am, absolutely knackered. We would be up early the next day, there were places to see and dives to do. After a hearty breakfast, I went and hired a mini bus with Derek so we could all get around together, visiting various dive sites.

Shortly after, we located the dive shop in Saint Pauls Bay and hired the cylinders and weights. Anna was the Dutch instructor at the shop and was quite attractive to say the least! She was very keen to embark on a night dive at some point in the week with us; I can only think it was our charisma that she was drawn to, as we firmed up a time and place for later in the week. The dive shop owner was still trying to persuade us to book a week's dive package with them but we declined their kind offer because Derek had been to Malta a few times and knew all the dive sites well, so off we went.

There were plenty of dive sites to choose from and I left it to Derek to decide which ones we should do. We arrived at a dive site one hot afternoon and after parking up at the top of the hill and kitting up, the sweat was pouring out of me. I just needed to get in to the water as quickly as possible. Derek and I were ready when Alan's cylinder just slid out of his harness. If it hadn't been so hot, it would have been hilarious. After calling him a few choice words, we got his cylinder back where it should be and staggered down to the water. The cooling effect was just the ticket and we were soon enjoying the clear waters of Malta. After just five minuets I had managed to put my hand down on to a spiny urchin; it hurt like hell, but nothing like fire coral. I took off my glove and managed to get the spine out and continued with the dive. I can't say it was exciting because it was just sand and sea grass but the water was crystal clear and cool, and all we had to do was find some decent dive locations.

On the third day, we caught the ferry across to Gozo where we planned to dive the Blue Hole. We parked the mini van on the volcanic rock and got out. The temperature was close to 38 degrees and there was a bit of a hike to the entry point, with dive cylinders in hand we climbed across the hot rock and after fifteen minuets and a bucket of sweat we were at the water's edge of the Blue Hole. I lay my tank down and just fell in the water to cool off - what a relief! After a cool off I kitted up, pulled on my fins, and dropped beneath the surface. It was like a giant goldfish bowl. We soon found ourselves at 57 metres with coloured fish all around us. This did have the wow factor for me and to top it all, we could swim down and out in to the open sea. I spent nearly an hour at various shallower depths, finning from point to point, finishing the dive back in the Blue Hole. It was a great, scenic dive.

After returning to the bus, we had some lunch and I took Kay for her first ever dive. For someone who had never dived before, she did great, but was honest enough to say it wasn't for her. It's like Marmite.

That night we were all in high spirits and Derek was looking at some dive sites for the next day. He was keen to find something to top the day's dive and the 60 metre dive he had done on a previous trip. The evening rolled on late in to the early hours. "I have a great idea", he announced, "Let's do a deep dive tomorrow. I know the location. We can head out on our own, nice and early and be back for lunch; and so the scene was set.

No sooner had my head hit the pillow, than my watch alarm was waking me. I quickly pulled on some clothes, grabbed my dive bag and was out the door. Derek was waiting at the van. "Nice day for it" was his welcome greeting, "Yeah, nice day" was my response. We set off; it was about 7.30 am and the roads were quite empty. We drove for nearly an hour and passed the time with a diving themed conversation on past dives and funny situations that had occurred. The mood was relaxed and light hearted.

Derek pulled the van up in to a desolate, rocky expanse of uneven rock and we got out. The sun was already high in the clear, blue sky and I could feel the heat burning my already sunburnt legs. We walked to the edge of the cliff and peered down at the open sea. Christ, is this the place? How do we get down there? I thought. Before I had the chance to ask, Derek pointed out the 160 random steps that zig zagged down through the cliff face. Right, let's get on with it before it gets any hotter.

We pulled on our 5 mm shorty wetsuits and strapped on our weight belts and tanks. After we locked the van, we headed for the steps. Apart from a local man fishing, we were the only people there. After the first tentative steps, we got in to a steady pace; down and down the steps, which seemed to go on and on. At about half way down we stopped for a breather and I glanced back up to where we had come from. Bloody Hell, it was going to be some ball ache getting back up those steps, but it was too late to worry about that now and we set off again down the remainder of the steps. We finally reached the bottom after nearly 15 minutes and dropped straight in to the sea just to cool off for 5 minutes.

After the short recovery, I checked my air was turned on and my US Diver regulator was in full working order. I could not afford any equipment failures as we were both only using single tanks, for the simple reason it would be impossible to carry two tanks each in one journey down those bloody steps. After the dive checks, we were ready to go. With a hiss of air vented from my buoyancy jacket, I disappeared under the surface. Derek was already a few feet ahead of me and so I followed after him, catching him up a few moments later. At about 18 metres, the water temperature changed from a warm 70 degrees, to what felt cold. On we went. The sea bed was devoid of any marine life and we were heading down a never ending shingle slope. I checked my computer on my right wrist: 40 metres. I glanced to my left to check Derek was OK. He glanced back and gave me the OK signal. I looked ahead of me and the water was clear and grey, matching the sea bed. This was due to the lack of natural sunlight at that depth.

Passing 50 metres, I felt absolutely fine. I was used to diving to those depths in the UK, where the water's dark and you would need a 50 watt torch just to see your dive gauges. In the time it took me to look left across to Derek and then ahead and back to my dive computer, I was at 65 metres and I could feel the effects of nitrogen narcosis. My brain was in some sort of dull, lethargic, trance and I wondered how deep we might get before we stopped. Again, I glanced at this person next to me. I could hear his bubbles pouring from his Poseidon regulator. I focussed back on my dive computer: 70 metres. I checked with myself "Am I still comfortable at this depth?" I was undecided and I was now at 75 metres. There was no end to the sloping sea bed I was following. The sound of the exhaled air from the regulators was all I could focus on. That's it. I slowed to a stop at 79 metres and stared blankly ahead realising I was in trouble. I had tunnel vision with green, cloudy patches in my vision. This was a new and frightening situation for me and although I had been in some challenging situations through out my diving career this was the big one, the one you know you shouldn't even be in, and it's all your own doing. The nightmare that you can't just wake up and say to yourself 'god, that was horrible', and get on with your day. My heart began to pound, I turned to Derek and I realised I had to end this dive right now. I turned around and started finning back up the slope that now looked like a wall. The green blotches and tunnel vision were all I could see and I was breathing heavily and I just couldn't think straight - mad panic gripped me. What had I done? My regulator fell from my mouth and I gulped a mouth full of sea water, but bizarrely it didn't taste of sea water, and some how I managed to avoid vomiting. I took hold of the regulator with my now clumsy uncoordinated hands and pushed it in the direction of my face whilst pushing the purge button at the front of the reg; bubbles of air erupted in my face and with more luck than skill the reg was back in my mouth. Cool air was forced in to my mouth and in to my lungs but as soon as I took my hands away from the reg my mouth was unable to make a water tight seal and I was now breathing a salt water air mix. My head was pounding by now and nothing was working. My coordination was failing. I was now fighting for my life.

I clamped my hand back across the front of my regulator holding it in my mouth just to make a seal and stop it falling from my mouth again; now I am not a religious man but I started praying to God that I didn't die.

My dive computer was bleeping like crazy and I knew I was ascending too fast, but I didn't have a choice. The regulator was incapable of delivering the amount of air I was now trying to draw from it and I was close to a black out. F**k, what have I done? What if I don't make it? What if Derek doesn't make it? What would I tell his family? My mind was now racing - the next 5 minutes seemed like a lifetime. A battle to stay in some sort of control of this life and death situation I had got myself in to. I kept finning up and up; the alarm ringing from my dive computer, the alarm bells and emotions racing round my head in my personal fight for life.

With tears in my eyes and thoughts of my demise, family, friends, and what would I tell the others if I should make it and Derek didn't, I realised that I might just get out of this with my life. I could feel my head pounding like I had a hangover from hell but I could now see and coordination had returned - the regulator was now firmly between my teeth and I was breathing within its limitations.

Having regained control at about 25 metres, I glanced around for Derek. He was 30 metres away, in mid water. I finned over in his direction and he signalled OK. I returned the OK and we made our way to a 6 metre spot in the sea and decompressed until I was out of air. Although I had made it up from 79 metres, it had not been controlled and my dive computer was still showing a rapid ascent, but when your air is out you have no choice but to surface and take your chances.

Back at the entry point, I was somewhat subdued and just chilled out for half an hour in relative silence, trying to gather my thoughts on this crazy, selfish, irresponsible situation I had put myself in. After a while Derek asked me what had happened down there and all I could say was that I had reached my limit and nearly killed myself in the process. That was the biggest lesson in diving I ever learnt; plan the dive, dive the plan and know your limitations.

We began the climb back up the 160 steps and I was mindful that if either of us got a bend we would be in big trouble out here in the middle of nowhere. After reaching the top without any symptoms, I felt a lot more confident that we would be fine and we were, but it would be a long time before I dived to those depths again and certainly not on air.

After that I was quite content to take it easy and the night dive with Anna, Derek and myself should be a walk in the park. It was dusk at the Inland Sea and after parking the van at the small bar Anna pulled up and we got kitted up and walked down to the water's edge. Although it was now close to 10 PM it was still quite light and the air was still warm from the searing heat of the day. We all had dive lights, and after some quick buddy checks we were in the cool Mediterranean water, exploring around the various rocks and fissures; it was quite different to diving this place in the day light, and there were octopus and moray eels in every crevice. Derek had the camera and was off ahead of us capturing the moments. We were at about Fifteen meters and it was completely black and our dive lights were the only means of visual orientation. Anna had stayed close by me for all of this dive, and we had been in the water for 25 minutes when I felt her grip my arm. This gave me a start; I quickly turned and shone my torch in her direction, her eyes were wide and she had the look of a scared rabbit caught in the headlights. I tried to reassure her with some hand signals, but it was hopeless and I quickly took her by the arm and we made our way to the surface. With her buoyancy compensator inflated we bobbed on the surface and waited for Derek. He surfaced shortly after and the three of us made our way back to terra firma. Anna was clearly shaken by the whole episode and became very emotional. To this day I have no idea what had spooked her, but as an instructor I certainly hadn't expected panic like that underwater. She thanked me for getting her to the surface and vowed not to dive at night again. She had discovered her diving limits for the time being. Then just to comfort the now emotional Anna I told her that I only rescued her because it was her round at the bar! She dried her eyes and we all had a well deserved drink.

Back in the UK, I caught sight of a TV programme about Malta and the Great White Shark that was caught just off on of the dive sites we had done last week! Kay and I just looked at each other in amazement; the thing is you just don't know what a game of chance we play.

Boats and ladders

It was diving as usual on all the great wrecks that I had been diving on over the past 11 years, although I had drifted away from Bristol Number Three Club. I had been concentrating on developing deeper diving on further afield wrecks.

Over the years, since the start of my diving, my dive gear got heavier as equipment was added: Extra cylinders, dive lights, lifting bags and wrecking tools. It was all evolving. The diving I was now involved in were deeper and further out from the shallower, closer wrecks I had started diving on in the early days.

The dives required greater planning, more dive equipment and back up, and the right vessel to do it from. The hard boat had the lot. Once the boat was booked, all that was left to do was choose the dive location, plan the dive time and best deco mix and turn up on the day. Once you had loaded yourself and all the diving equipment aboard, all that was left to do was sit back and enjoy the ride out to the dive site.

It was all down to the skipper to get you out there, locate the wreck, secure the shot line to it and tell you when slack water had settled over the wreck. If the skipper got it wrong, you could end up on a pile of sand or be pulled from the wreck by the strength of the current. Thankfully, we had good, seasoned skippers.

I had a close number of dive mates and when I put together various dive trips throughout the years, I had no trouble filling the other places on the boat. We all had a great passion for diving and were totally committed and when I had no dives of my own booked, I could join my mates on their trips. It was a perfect way of doing new wrecks and trusty old ones.

The hard boats were varied according to the dive site and wreck location. You had to be prepared to travel and get up early if you wanted to dive with the big boys, as they say.

It was late in the year of 1994 and I was now diving with a full set of tech dive equipment using Nitrox as a deco gas mix, my twin 15 litre main tanks and two 7 litre decompression tanks containing mixes up to 80% oxygen. This would speed up the decompression time I had to spend in the water. All this equipment weighed a staggering 13 stone. I was fit as a butcher's dog, humping this lot around up and down the jetty, on and off the boat, and let's not forget the dreaded ladder to get back on board the boat.

I was diving off a hard boat one summer's day, off the coast of Weymouth. I had been in the water for over an hour and had forgotten how heavy the kit on my back actually was. I grabbed hold of the ladder and began to climb it rung by rung. The ladder was made of scaffolding, welded together on a central spine with alternate rungs either side. It was about 8 feet high and attached to the side of the boat. As I climbed it, the weight on my back got heavier and heavier, until all 13 stone was being supported by my legs. Just as I reached the deck line of the boat, my foot slipped off the side of the ladder rung and I slid right back in to the water with the speed of a bomb falling from the sky. How my face did not hit the ladder as I hurtled down, I will never know. I must have been a lucky bastard that day. Then I had to start all over again with even more tired legs. I was determined not to fall again, mainly because by now, the rest of the divers were all looking down at me with great amusement on their faces. I gritted my teeth and hauled myself up successfully, no more of that nonsense. Although the skipper couldn't resist a photo of me struggling up his ball breaking ladder. He had plans for me: two weeks later, my picture was on his stand at the dive show in Birmingham promoting his charter boat business - technical divers welcome. Some people never miss an opportunity.

Free flow

In the winter of 1994, Darren and I had decided to go diving at Stony Cove, in Leicester. We would drive up early and try out some new kit. We had to get there before 6.30 am to secure a parking space at the bottom car park. It was that popular in the winter months, when the weather was too rough to dive out in the sea.

We set off at 4 am and got there just after 6 am. We parked and got kitted up ready for the dive. I was diving with twin 15s and Poseidon regulators. In the diving world, they are regarded as one of the best regulators you can buy. I am inclined to agree, but they are sensitive in cold water and can free flow at an alarming rate. The water temperature was at 4 degrees and we were using argon for suit inflation. The reasoning behind this was that argon is an inert gas that is denser than air and would give it greater thermal properties than just air.

There were various things to look at, pieces of aircraft, old cars and other random things. We opted for what is called the hydra box. It was a 15ft square steel box that you could enter from underneath and as you exhaled, the spent gas from your regulator filled the top of the box. After 4 minutes, the water got forced out and you could remove you reg and chat to your fellow diver whilst breathing the air space you had created, but not for long. I removed my reg and Darren did the same. We exchanged some conversation. I returned the regulator to my mouth and took a breath. It immediately went in to free flow. That is when air pours from the reg and you can't stop it. I quickly checked my gauge; I had nearly 200 bar and I made my exit from the box. Once outside, I switched over to my other reg that was connected to the other 15 litre cylinder. I checked the gauge on the free flowing reg and there was only 50 bar left in it. That was one Hell of a free flow. Had I only had one cylinder, I would have had a problem that would have had to be sorted by air sharing with Darren, 34 metres back to the surface.

I signalled to Darren I was OK and we made our way back to the surface. Back at the pontoon, we carried out a deco stop. All was under control and the argon had done a great job of keeping us warm; shame it couldn't help the regulator. Once back at the car, we had a chat about the free flow and neither of us could comprehend how quickly it had emptied the cylinder. It just confirmed to us both how important it was to carry a complete separate system, just in case of this sort of situation.

Although I dive a lot, these sorts of failures keep you on your toes and remind you that you are in an alien world and you are just visiting it for a limited amount of time.

The wrecks of Scapa Flow

In April 1995 I found myself heading back to Scapa Flow and although I had been up there a few times by now, I was still excited about it. Dave and Sandra had organised the trip and I must say it was nice when someone else did all the organising on a trip like this.

I knew the 12 people that were on the trip; Richard Bull, from Current State Diving, was meant to be coming but had to back out at the last minute due to business commitments. It was a bit of a shame, but he had found someone to fill his place, so all was well on the financial side and there were an even number of divers, so everyone would have a buddy. His replacement, Alan, was a competent diver and instructor and that was the important thing. We all travelled up independently, meeting at Thurso in the early hours of Saturday morning.

I was sharing a lift with Darren my regular dive buddy and due to the amount of kit, that's all we could get in my Mondeo. We were on the road at 5 am and were making good time when we got a call. Alan had not arrived on time for his lift and no one had his telephone number. Well, he was Richard's replacement choice, so there was only one thing for it, Darren called Rich Bull. It was 5.30 am. Rich answered in a half asleep manner. It took Darren 5 minutes to get Richard to understand why he was ringing him. We got Alan's number and passed it back to his lift. That's all sorted, or so we thought. At about 10 am, we were at Birmingham and pulled in for a respite and some breakfast. Tucking in to a Little Chef Magnificent 7, we called to see where the others were. It beggars belief. Alan had got to the rendezvous for his lift. They set off late and at Cheltenham he realised he'd forgotten his drysuit and had to get his missus to drive to Cheltenham with it. I don't think he was very popular at that moment. I looked at Darren and we just had a smile. It could happen to anyone, but there were always some guys that would be top of that list.

We polished off our breakfast and got back on the road. Hour after hour we drove, arriving at Thurso late evening.
After a late night and some broken sleep, we ate breakfast and waited for the ferry. At 11.30 am, we were on it and spirits were high. We didn't know it yet, but two people were going to have the dive of their lives.

We disembarked from the ferry and walked around the quay to find our boat, *MV Sunrise*. She'd not changed a bit and nor had the skipper, Mark and his wife Debbie. They were still great hosts. Darren and I quickly got our sleeping bags and clothes down to our preferred bunks, because on a small boat with limited space, not all bunks are the same size and when you will be spending a week on board, with late nights and early starts, you will want to make the best of what time you spend sleeping. Comfort is king and size does matter. Our bunk was the first one at the bottom of the ladder, leading off the upper saloon and main living area. I was on the top bunk with Darren on the lower. There were no port holes in any of the bunk rooms which was probably just as well because Darren would be trying to remove them. Old habits die hard.

Once we had our sleeping quarters sorted, it was time to get the dive kit on board and prepare for the first dive on the Sunday. I would be using the dive boat's 12 litre cylinders, twinning them up with a 7 litre for deco and of course my trusty dive lights. After an hour, I was sorted and so off to the Ferry Inn for a steak dinner. After the meal, we headed to the Royal Oak for 1 last beer, before long it was midnight and time to head back to the boat and hit the sack.

Sunday morning 7am, the alarm woke me from my slumber. It was bloody typical, Darren had been snoring most of the night and he only shut up a few hours ago. Of course, I don't snore; well that's what I tell myself. I swilled my face, cleaned my teeth and headed up the stairs to have some toast and tea. A few of the others were already up. Everyone was in good sprits and looking forward to the first dive of the week.

We were all well seasoned divers and so we were going to get straight in to the week's diving with a dive on one of the light cruisers, the *Brummer*, lying in 36 metres of water, on her side. She was built in 1916 by AG Vulcan and had a water displacement of 4,308 tons. She had twin turbines and twin propellers and was capable of achieving speeds of 28 knots, which was quick for the day. She measured 462 feet with a beam of 44 feet and had a draught of nearly 20 feet.

She was built for speed and was only lightly armoured, to keep her weight down. Crewed by 309 men, she saw action in the wars, disrupting convoys between Norway and Britain.

After tea and toast I heard the engine start and we gently pulled out of the harbour in to the main flow. Although it was a vast expanse of sheltered water, it could be quite rough with a large swell. Back in 1914, the British used this place as the main anchorage for the Royal Navy's home fleet. Great warships like *HMS Vanguard, HMS Royal Oak* and *HMS Hampshire* had used the anchorage for refuelling and as a base to set out on major task force operations during the wars.

Back on the *Sunrise,* in the bow area we all got kitted up. The deck had been covered in with an aluminium roof to keep us warm and dry between dives. The only down side to this was it was not quite high enough for a 6 foot tall person, so you had to try and remember not to stand up quickly. We all took turns on finding out just how unforgiving the roof was.

I was diving with Darren and we were the second pair to enter the water, but as with most first dives, not everyone was ready and Alan's dive buddy had jumped in minus a weight belt, so he teamed up with us.

The *Brummer* lies at a depth of 36 metres on her starboard side. Darren had two 50 watt halogen bulbs in his hand crafted underwater lights and there was so much light from them, I didn't even bother to switch my own lights on. The visibility in the water was good at about 8 metres and large sections of the wreck could be distinguished with little effort or imagination. As we dropped down in to the mid section of the wreck, I spotted a large port hole that was fixed in to a steel bulkhead. I had a quick inspection of it and came to the conclusion that this port hole would not be coming back to the surface with me on this dive or anyone else's dive for that matter. These ships had been underwater for over 70 years and their steel was still very solid and not ravaged much by rust or corrosion.

Finning along an external corridor, we passed some large J cylinders secured to a wall. They still had paint on them. It was a true testament to time and the quality that these ships were built to. Darren turned to me and I was dazzled by the lights. I raised my hand to shield my eyes and he quickly got the picture and covered them with his hand. My eyes quickly readjusted to the light and we checked our dive computers. We were in to 8 minutes decompression. I signalled to Alan, and the 3 of us began our ascent to the surface. We stopped at 6 metres and carried out our deco stop. We all hung in suspension effortlessly and in complete control. We were all accomplished divers and it had become almost second nature to us in this underwater world. After the 8 minutes we stopped at 3 metres for just 2 minutes. We had been in the water for 38 minutes and it had been a good dive. On the surface I could see the boat turning to port and arcing round in our direction. There was just a small swell and within 4 minutes we were alongside the boat. I took hold of the ladder and clambered up it, finding a suitable seating spot on the deck. After pulling off my mask and hood I heard the other divers talking excitedly about the dive. One of the other divers gave me a hand to get my tanks off and I set them aside ready for filling for the next dive. Before the afternoon dive, there was just time for me to finish cooking breakfast as I was on catering duty.

The option of self catering was saving us all £300, plus I got to dive first, so that I was out first to carry on cooking brekkie. Well, that was the theory anyway and there were no shortage of willing helpers, so it was pretty easy as far as I was concerned.

The galley was small, but well equipped. Full size gas cooker, sink and limited work top space, so as 2 breakfasts were plated up, someone took them out of the way, so there was room to plate up 2 more.

Planning was every thing and I had it down to a fine art. The day before, I would boil up some potatoes ready for frying in the morning. As my old boss would say, it's just as easy to cook a bad breakfast as it is to cook a good one and I skimped on nothing. There was bacon, sausage, beans, tomatoes, toast, fried bread, eggs and of course, fried potatoes, bread and butter and gallons of tea. If there's one thing diving does for you, it is give you a massive appetite and as the cook, I couldn't have divers complaining that they were hungry on my shift.

After breakfast we headed off to visit the museum. Mark moored the boat up and we stepped off the deck on to the concrete mooring. There was not much to see; it was a barren wasteland with rusting pieces of abandoned machinery and discarded pieces of steel drums and other random things. Although the sun was out, the wind was blowing hard and it felt cold. After a 10 minute brisk walk, we were in the grounds of the museum. One of the most striking sights to first catch my eye was the massive 3 bladed phosphorus bronze propeller that had been removed from the armoured cruiser *HMS Hampshire*.

Alongside it were guns of various sizes from various wrecks and as they were made from thick armour plate we were able to climb on them for various photo backdrops.

Inside the museum, there were the original pumps and heaters that pumped oil to our Atlantic fleet of ships during both wars. The oil itself was so thick that it had to be heated so that it would be thin enough to be pumped out to some of our biggest battleships like the *Royal Oak* and the *Hampshire* to name a few. It was quite a piece of bygone engineering with its highly polished brass bearings and crank shafts. It was so well maintained that it looked like it could be back in service at the touch of a button. Walking out of the pump house I spotted a semi dismantled torpedo. Its size took me by surprise as I hadn't thought they were that big, even though these devices had sunk thousands of ships between the two World Wars.

Around the corner there were a large number of salvaged items: ships bells, navigation lights, port holes, shell cases and hand guns. It was like an Aladdin's cave that any diver would be proud to have as their collection. Well, I had seen all I could and it was time to get back to the dive boat and get ready for a cup of tea and the afternoon dive on the *Dresden*.

With the *Sunrise* underway to the *Dresden*, I pulled on my drysuit and sorted out my cylinders. My buddy and I were sat ready to dive 5 minutes before we reached the dive site. The skipper gave us the signal and we stepped off the side of the boat and in to the water. With a few kicks of my fins I had hold of the buoy that marked the dive location. With a quick signal to Darren, I vented some air and headed down the shot line that was attached to the wreck 30 metres down, on the sea bed. The water visibility was at least 10 metres and as I took a look at my dive computer to check my depth, it read 12 metres and I could see the shape of the cruiser.

With the bow and her stern very much intact I could make out large sections and individual features. The anchor chains were run out and fallen silently to the sea bed 10 metres from the capstan. I finned up to the top of the bow that was in only 16 metres of water. This would give us a longer time down on the wreck. As we finned back towards the stern, we soon reached the mid section and Darren dropped down in to the mass of twisted metal and hanging cables. He must have been about 10 metres away from me and I had no trouble seeing him, the visibility was as good as I could have wished for. I carried on finning and we started heading for the stern where both gun turrets still sat in place. We checked our dive time and it was time to head up to the surface. Glancing to my right, I spotted the stern shot line and we both ascended it, carrying out our deco stops as we went. It certainly made a difference when the water was that clear and you had the shot line to carry out your ascent and deco stops on. Back aboard the *Sunrise,* we were very pleased with the dive and so were the rest of the divers. If the rest of the week was as good as today, we were in for a damn good week's diving.

With the last of the divers up and back onboard, Mark pointed the boat back to Stromness. We would be spending the night back in port so there would be a chance to walk up through the main street and visit some pubs before dinner. The shops were just what you would expect from a small island community. Not a great deal of choice, higher prices, but very friendly people running them; nothing was too much trouble.

Once the boat was moored up and Mark had 240 volt electrics back on the boat, we could all charge up our lights ready for the following day. Some of the other divers had already left the boat to go to the pub and so we would probably catch up with them at some point later in the evening. Darren, Ian, Gary and yours truly headed off to the Royal Hotel for a few pints of 80 Shillings bitter. Once in the pub, we were lucky enough to get a table next to the coal fire that was blazing in the hearth. We were all in high spirits and chatted over the day's diving and of the dives to come. As with most holidays there were lots of thing to do and insufficient time to cover it, so planning was essential.

When time is short it pays to choose wisely and although we had all been up here before, some wrecks were better than others. We were all in agreement about the big battleships in that although they are massive, there was not a huge amount to see on them, especially if you didn't hit the right spot, first time when you got down to them, as I had experienced on a previous dive.

There were three main battleships, The *Markgraf, Konig* and the *Kron Prince Wilhelm*. All three were upside down in 40 metres plus and were lying at an angle either to port or starboard. They were so heavy, at over 25,000 tonnes, that they were buried in the sea bed at an angle up to their hulls. All of the super structure sat in the mud, with just a small amount to be seen on the raised side of the higher angle and nothing to see on the deeper one.

I had dived one a few years ago and the shot line took me over the wrong side and into a wall of featureless hull and a sandy sea bed. As soon as I knew I was on the wrong side my buddy and I made our way back, but by the time we had retraced our steps we had run out of time and had to end the dive and trust we had better luck next time.

With talk of big wrecks the conversation got around to some prestigious wrecks like the *Royal Oak, Vanguard* and *HMS Hampshire*. Well, we knew we wouldn't be allowed to dive the *Oak* or the *Vanguard*, that went without saying, but the *Hampshire*, well that was a possible. Slim, but possible. She was in 64 metres of water, a few miles off the coast at Marwick Head, far enough away from the eyes of the Royal Navy. All I had to do was persuade our skipper to put us on it. I would have to pick my moment.

The pub was packed with locals and other divers. There was a new charter boat in operation, doing mixed gas courses and offering the qualified divers the chance to visit some of the deeper, less dived wrecks. The divers on this boat tended to keep themselves to themselves, it was as if we were not worthy of their presence and so didn't engage in conversation with us. Not that it particularly bothered us as we had bigger fish to fry, so we headed off to the Ferry Inn for some food. It was a good job I was not watching my weight. After a 16 oz steak and Garlic Bread, I headed back to the boat for some well needed shut eye. Back on board, Dave, Sandra and the others were watching TV, discussing the planned dives for the following day. I was not too bothered what I did tomorrow, but I had a plan for something later in the week and left them to it.

Up bright and early the next day I sat myself down in the lounge and poured myself a cup of tea. Dave Gould briefed me on the plan. We were going to dive the wreck of the *Karlsruhe* and we needed to be on site for 8.30 am. The engine fired up and Mark manoeuvred out of the mooring and in to the flow. Again the weather was good, flat calm with just a gentle breeze. I had kitting up time down to a fine art and so I just needed 15 minutes and I was ready to go, so there was no great rush. I just needed to put the sausages, bacon and beans on the stove because I was still on breakfast duty.

We would be diving the wreck of the *Inverlane* in the afternoon and spending the night moored up at Burray along with 2 other dive boats. Mark had reserved us a table for dinner and it was to be a late and lively night.

The skipper shouted down 20 minutes to dive site time, to get out of the galley and in to my drysuit and ready to dive. Darren and I would be first, as usual. Mark shouted "Ready first pair?"

We were ready to go and off the side, keeping a firm hand on our face masks and demand valves when we jumped as it was about a 6 feet drop in to the sea and you could easily lose a mask or the demand valve out of your mouth; not a good start to any dive.

At a depth of 8 metres, I could see the wreck. The visibility was great. My buddy was now rummaging through the open port side of this cruiser and I was at least 12 metres away from him looking at something else. The *Karlsruhe* was lying in just 26 metres of water on her starboard side. She was a lighter ship than the *Koln* and the *Dresden* and was capable of 28 knots when her two oil/coal fired turbines were at full capacity. Her armaments were adequate, two anti aircraft guns, eight 5.9 inch single gun turrets and two deck mounted torpedo tubes. She was 12 metres proud of the sea bed and only 12 metres from the surface. It was so light down there I didn't need to turn on my torch, there was enough light from the surface to see the massive amounts of salvaging that had taken place on her. It was a good old rummage dive. Finning through the wreckage I got to the stern area that was the most intact. There were lots of hatchways to explore and I entered some of the larger ones and found large gears and machinery, it looked like it could be part of the engine room. I didn't linger too long in the confined spaces because every time you touched or moved, silt bellowed up from everywhere and the visibility dropped to zero. Finning back up to the port side of the stern, we took the opportunity to explore as this was the most intact section of the wreck. There was a large hole that had been blasted in the hull where there were large cogs visible. This 5,354 tonne cruiser was quite a dive, but we now had to fin back the way we had come, but at a shallower depth, viewing the starboard side of the hull where various large holes appeared. Peering in them, they seemed inviting, but we resisted temptation as our dive time was almost over and we needed to head for the surface.

I could see the shot line and we were soon heading up it to the surface. Once our decompression penalties had been paid in various stops on our ascent, we surfaced and waited for the boat to pick us up. It drew alongside us. I grabbed the ladder and began to climb. It didn't get any easier the more times you climbed it and with twin 12 litre cylinders on my back it was tough on the old legs. Once on board, it was good to sit down and take the weight off.

I got out of my dive gear and back down in to the galley to sort out breakfast for the hungry dozen. We had got fried mash potatoes this morning. I must say, one of my favourites with a cooked brekkie.

I was now just chilling out, waiting for the dive on the block ship *Inverlane*. This ship was built in 1938 in West Germany as a 9,000 tonne tanker and was damaged by a mine off the coast of South Shields in 1939.

She was made watertight and towed to Scapa Flow and sunk in Burray Sound. The idea behind this was to keep the U boats out of the Flow. The plan was to dive her at slack water and then get inside her from the top of the bow section of the wreck that was protruding out of the water. At 2.30 pm, we pulled alongside her and I jumped on to her deck to secure our boats bow line to the wreck. It was now just a case of kitting up and walking off the deck of the *Sunrise* to the deck of the *Inverlane*, but just before we kitted up, we were going to have a team photo.

With the photo taken, I kitted up and walked over to the large hatchway in her deck. It didn't look so big now I had all my kit on. Nevertheless, I stepped forward and plunged in to the hatchway. There were different deck levels with ladders and doorways to fin up, down and through. The water was as clear as gin and with a shallow depth of less than 10 metres, I spent over an hour just exploring this old wreck. I thought slack water had come and gone during this time because I had just swum past a large hole leading out to the open sea and it had slammed me in to the opposite steel wall and held me there. If the waters force had been from the other direction, I would have been jettisoned completely from the wreck and lost in the tidal flow.

The dive made a nice change from some of the main wrecks and even the skipper, Mark, got to have a dive on her. With all of us back on board, we headed in to Burray for the night.

After 10 minutes steam, we approached the mooring. There were already two other boats tied up, so we tied off to the nearest one we came to. After getting ourselves sorted out ready for the diving the next day, we all headed off to the pub. It didn't take long to get a pool tournament going and after a well deserved drink of 80 Shillings we were swapping stories with the divers from the two other boats and playing pool. The evening rolled on at a bit of a pace. I was at the bar chatting to our skippers mate from one of the other boat, and as I remember, it went something like this:

"So Keith, have you been out to dive the *Hampshire* recently?", "Yeah, but it was a few years ago and we kept it very quiet. The MOD is not keen on divers diving on war graves even if they just look and don't touch. If a skipper is found to have artefacts on board from a war grave, the penalties are severe. Equipment and even the boat can be impounded and it's not to be treated lightly". "OK Keith, that's fair enough. Would you be prepared to take 4 of us out to the dive site this week?", "Well, I may Dave, but you ought to give Mark the opportunity first. It would be a bit undermining of me to just agree to take you" and I could see his point, even after six or seven pints of Orkney's finest, but I had asked Mark on previous trips and he had always dismissed it. I had learnt to accept it, but I had my mind set on it this time, and with or without Mark, I was going to dive this legendary wreck if I had a chance.

Dive the Hampshire

I left Keith at the bar and had a quiet word in Darren's ear about the conversation that I had just had with Keith. "So Dave, are you going to ask him now?" Darren said, his pint now at rest on the table. "Well I may as well as we have got naff all to lose". Mark was now at the bar chatting to Keith, so I took my chance and approached them. Mark was in good spirits and having a joke with Keith. I waited for a pause in their banter and began my pitch.

Mark listened to me as I presented my case and I could tell he was none too keen on the whole idea, but he said he would sleep on it and let me know. Well, at least it wasn't a no. As I headed back to Darren, I told him that he was going to think about it, so we should see what happened and just enjoy the rest of the evening. The drinks kept coming and the finale was a Viking cup filled with a punch of various spirits supplied by our respective skippers. I took a sip and it nearly took my head off and I think it is fair to say it would sort the men from the boys, so when the Viking helmet came around again, some passed it by. Never mind, all the more for the men. We finally hit the sack back on the boat at about 2 am, all very happy, but tired.

At 7 am there was movement aboard the *Sunrise* and bleary eyed people began sorting out their breakfast before getting in to their dive suits and the first dive of the day. Most of us had hangovers. That included Mark, our skipper. Just as well, because he played a part in our hangovers bringing out that Viking hat full of various spirits.

We would be diving the *Karlsure*. She was in quite a shallow depth and we would have a good dive time on her. As usual, Darren and I were over the side first and the visibility was 10 metres plus. We rummaged around the mid section and found some electrical terminals attached to brass mounts. Darren sent them to the surface; we would collect anything back in the day. Continuing on, wires and debris were hanging every where and we took care not to get snagged. Moving aft, the stern part of the wreck appeared to be in much better condition and we spent the last ten minutes peering through hatches before shooting the SMB and making our ascent.

Back on board we were more than ready for our breakfast. I quickly got out of my drysuit and headed down to the galley to dish up the food. We had got fried potatoes with the fry up this morning; it should soak up the drinks from last night and keep us going until dinner. Later, after we had all eaten, Jimmuck attended to the filling of our cylinders. I had chosen a 36% Nitrox fill as the dive was on a shallow block ship and the mix would help get rid of the hangover that refused to go away. I was flagging and I needed all the help I could muster.

I had got 3 hours before the dive and I found a comfy spot in the saloon and drifted off to sleep. The whole mood on the boat was a bit subdued; I couldn't understand why!! At 2.30 pm, I was back in my drysuit and poised to leap in to the sea. This particular wreck had a lot of sea life on her and we would spend the entire dive inside her, avoiding the strong current outside.

As the buoy got closer, Darren and I stepped over the side and dropped in to the water, quickly descending the shot line attached to the wreck. As anticipated, we swam in to the wreck and the visibility was 15 metres and virtually without any tidal current. It was a good, easy dive with lots to see. After 40 minutes we headed out to make our ascent. I quickly looked around and located the shot line and made my way up it. I could see the hull of our boat from the sea bed, so the visibility must have been at least 16 metres. Once on the surface, I signalled to the dive boat and waited to be picked up. The sea was almost flat calm with just a light breeze. They were ideal diving conditions. As the 70 ft dive boat slowed to pick us up, I grabbed the ladder and climbed back on board. Dave had made tea and no sooner had I sat down with my dive kit removed when I had a hot cup of tea in my hand. You don't tend to get this kind of service on every dive trip.

With all back on board, the skipper swung the boat around and we headed back to Stromness for the evening. I thought we were eating out tonight, so I guessed I'd have a big steak.

I hadn't given much thought to my conversation I had with Mark the previous night. The diving had been just great and there had not been a moment to think. I just checked over my dive equipment as usual and got my tanks filled with a top off of air. After analysing them, I was left with a mix of 26%. That would be just fine for a 26 metre dive on one of the cruisers, which seemed to be the loose plan for the diving the following day. With my kit all checked, it was off to the shower room for a quick wash and brush up before dinner at the local pub, the Ferry Inn. Darren and a few others headed over to the pub and Ian got the first round in. We were offered a table for dinner, service was prompt and our steaks arrived within 20 minutes of ordering. As usual, they were excellent prime Aberdeen Angus medium rare, or as Ian says, "Whip its horns off and wipe its ass. That's what you call rare".

Within an hour, we had eaten and had moved from the dining area to the bar - it was packed, filled with dozens of divers all chatting and laughing loudly. Mark, the skipper, had just walked in and I bought him a pint of 80 Shillings as this was his favourite tipple (and ours). I would be diving on a nice shallow cruiser in the morning, or so I thought, when out of the blue, Mark asked me if I still wanted to dive the *Hampshire*. It took a few seconds for this to register, "What are you saying Mark?" was my reply. All of a sudden I became very focussed. "Well Dave", he replied, "We have a weather window tomorrow and if you want to dive the *Hampshire* it will have to be tomorrow. There will be some conditions: no one is to lift any artefacts off the wreck. If I see a lift bag it will be sent back to the wreck and I will not be happy as my livelihood depends on me staying within the law and working with the locals. This wreck is a war grave and it's only the fact that she lies some miles off Marwick Head and a fair distance from the eyes of the MOD that we can take a chance at bending the rules and diving her". "OK Mark, that sounds fine. Just give me a minute and I will let you know how many of us want to dive".

I wandered over to Darren, Ian, Gary and Alan, "Hey guys, who wants to take a shot at diving the *Hampshire* tomorrow?", "You're joking?" Ian replied, "No, it's on for those that want to do it. So, are you up for it or what?", "Yeah, we are up for it!" So there were 5 of us. I walked back over to Mark and told him.

So, "What's the plan?" they asked. We would be leaving the dock at 7 am for the long journey out to the wreck site. She lies at a depth of 65 metres, nearly 200 feet. Quite a depth to dive on just air, but this was all we had to hand. Mark had suggested we kept it quiet because if word got out and the MOD got involved, Mark would have had to cancel it. We understood the position clearly and headed back to the boat, to plan the dive.

Dave and a few others were not keen to dive this deep or for us to dive it either, but we were grown men and capable of making our own decisions on a dive of this calibre. We asked him to just accept we were experienced divers and were capable of attempting to dive this deep. If we felt uncomfortable at that depth, we would abort the dive. He came round to the idea that we weren't mad and Hell bent on some suicidal mission.

I took myself off to bed and my mind was racing, full of thoughts on the forthcoming dive. Eventually I fell asleep and woke to the sound of the *Sunrise* engine as Mark got underway. I got up straight away. I needed to change my dive cylinder configuration and work out a dive plan based on depth and bottom time. I was not the only one up early with things to do.

With the boat's engine already running, Darren, Ian, Gary and Alan were also up, as the boat pulled out of Stromness. The sun was just coming up and the water was like glass. The conditions looked perfect.

I headed down to the bottom deck where my dive kit had slept overnight. I had decided to dive with two twelve litre tanks and a deco mix of 50 % oxygen, using the Buhlman Navy Diver decompression tables. It took me just over 20 minutes to change tanks and re configure my kit to suit the impending dive. The other guys were doing the same. Dave had taken up the role of dive support which was greatly appreciated. There was not a lot for us to do now, but wait. We had quite a few hours before we would get out to the site.

Darren and I were out back on deck and the mood was quiet and focused, almost sombre. We looked out over the sea and it was still like glass with just a light breeze. We were drinking apple juice, just to hydrate ourselves as it was important not to dive dehydrated. Jimmuck, Mark's helper, was tying off a 56 lb piece of steel to a huge reel of nylon rope that we would use to drop on the wreck so that we could travel down it and on to the wreck.

The wreck of the *Hampshire* is in 68 metres of water, 1.5 miles from Marwick Head. She was built in Chatham Dockyard, Kent between 1902 and 1904 and launched in to service where she saw action in the battle of Jutland and joined tours to the Mediterranean and Far East. She was lost in a gale on 5th June 1916, after striking a mine.

As we got within 2 miles of the dive site, the 5 of us started to get kitted up. It had been a long wait and we were all a bit on edge and somewhat quiet. Even the other seven divers that were not diving were quiet. Dave and a few others were down on the dive deck assisting us as we kitted up. Darren and I were sat kitted up, opposite the entry point, looking out across the horizon. All I could see was the vast expanse of the sea. There was no land visible from anywhere on the boat and the sky was a dull grey. Word came down to us that we had arrived and it was just a matter of locating the wreck and dropping the shot on her. Ten minutes passed and I was wondering, "What if Mark can't find it?", but I needn't have worried. Just then, Dave came down and told us we were hooked in to the wreck and it was time to dive.

To say I was apprehensive would be the understatement of the year. I looked at Darren and we just did the "Let's do it" thing. We both stood up and waddled over to the entry point at the side of the boat. Looking out, the sky was dark and the sea an inky black. The white, 25 litre plastic drum that was attached to the shot line now hooked in to the wreck, rose and fell with the sea swell and slight chop that had now developed on it. I placed the regulator in my mouth and as the boat passed alongside the white drum, I stepped off the boat and finned towards it with Darren to my left side and the other three behind us. As we reached the drum, I couldn't help feeling a little bit small and insignificant in this vast expanse of water, miles from land, out in the deep Atlantic. We did a last minute check and then slipped beneath the surface.

As I descended, head first down the shot line, I could tell we were going to be in for a great experience and adrenalin pulsed through my body. The shot line was disappearing down and out in to the abyss at a semi horizontal angle. This made the decent very gradual, although I could see at least 20 metres ahead of me. I checked my depth, 20 metres. Darren was to my right side, just behind me. My exhaust bubbles gently flowed from my regulator and I felt very confident that I would see this through. I checked again, 38 metres, then 48 metres. I still felt good about the dive. I got my first sight of this mighty ship, the bow shape looked quite small, almost like a model, with it's long, thin shot line floating up from it in to my hands. I felt connected and yes, I guess I was a bit narked, my old friend nitrogen narcosis, but as I passed 58 metres, who wouldn't be. The bow was looming up like a massive v shaped jumble of twisted wreckage, no more than two or three metres proud of the sea bed. Yes, I was going to make it down and touch this piece of history. At 64 metres, I let go of the shot line and dropped down and rested on the side of this mighty battleship, waiting for Darren and the others to join me. One minute later, Darren joined me and we surveyed the wreck and surroundings.

Although the time we would spend on this wreck would be brief, you could take an awful lot in during a short time. The other three divers failed to show and looking back up the shot line, there was no sight of them. The visibility was 20 metres plus, the water was clear and to my surprise I did not even need my torch switched on. I looked down at the sandy sea bed. Just two or three metres away, lying in the sand, was a port hole with just a light dusting of sand over it, a dining plate and a toilet. All of these artefacts were undamaged and ready to be sent to the surface with the minimum of fuss, but we had promised Mark we would refrain from this action. I glanced over to my right and there was a huge section of superstructure, a doorway was open and beckoned to me. I held firm on what I had agreed and resisted the temptation to enter this war grave that was the resting place for 643 men, including Lord Kitchener. The other surprising thing about this wreck was the fact that there appeared to be very little marine growth covering it. I turned to Darren and we shook hands whilst on the wreck and then it was time to make our ascent back up the shot line and to the safety of the surface. I changed over regulators and put some air in to my jacket, in order to get some buoyancy. It's surprising how much air you have to use, just to get you buoyant and on the move towards the surface. With a bit more air and some leg work I was finally on the move up the shot line, with Darren close on my heels.

As I ascended, I kept looking back down at the wreck, savouring these last visual moments of the dive. As I slowed to a near stop at 57 metres, I could get a clear view of the bow. It looked like the deck, flat, but with no recognisable deck features. Of course, there wouldn't be, this wreck was upside down and the whole of the bow hull had been blown off. That's why she went down in just 15 minutes after hitting the mine.

I continued to ascend, and at 48 metres I could still make her out. What a dive. They don't get much better than this. I looked up the shot line, still no sign of the other three divers. I was assuming we would catch up with them at our shallower decompression stops and at 9 metres we did. They were all OK, but they didn't make it to the wreck which was a bit of a shame for them, but they did the right thing in aborting the dive due to its depth. I personally felt like a dog with two dicks and later Darren said the same. After some minutes, we levelled off at 6 metres to finish off our deco, but as we reached this depth, we found ourselves at 3 metres one minute, then back down to 7 and 8 metres. It was impossible to carry out a controlled decompression stop of fifteen minutes. We had no choice and dropped down to 9 metres. We could feel the shot line being pulled tight and then slackening off, but at least we were at a steady depth and not being pulled up and down like yo yo's. The deco would just take a bit longer and the longer we stayed, the rougher the surface conditions were getting.

After 35 minutes, with our deco completed, we headed for the surface. At five metres, I found myself in two metres a few seconds later. Hell, it must be bad on the surface and it was. Once on the surface, I was shocked by the conditions. The 70 feet converted fishing boat we called home was battling through a force 8 gale and a 15 feet swell. One minute I could see her, the next, nothing. This scenario happened time after time, with the boat getting closer and closer. I knew Mark was a good skipper and he would get us out of the water, but it wouldn't be easy. Dave was standing at the top of the ladder and he signalled one at a time. I watched as the boat got closer and I thought if this goes wrong and the boat hit me it would be really bad, but there was little time for worrying as the boat was now at my side. I took hold of the ladder and held on. Dave got a rope around my tanks and I took hold of the top rung of the ladder. As the boat pitched down on her port side, the sea was level with the dive deck. Then with the next surge, the sea lifted me and the boat deck clear of the water and Dave and Keith pulled me on to the dive deck. Then they tied me to a firm anchor point on the boat in case I was swept back over board whilst they got me out of my dive tanks. I began to feel sea sick; I had only been aboard 2 minutes.

As help arrived, I was de kitted, whilst Dave got ready for the next diver. One by one, we were all pulled back safely on board. I crawled in to the saloon. It looked like a hurricane had been through it. There was nothing left standing apart from the tables as they were bolted to the floor. As I made my way through to the galley for a deserved cup of tea, I asked where all the rest of the divers were and was told sea sickness had taken hold of them. I could certainly appreciate that, it was having a similar effect on me and I had only been back on board for 15 minutes. Jimmuck thought it was hilarious and went about trying to retrieve the shot line. After two attempts, Mark had had enough and decided to leave it and get his boat and us out of this deteriorating situation without incident or accident. I, for one, was happy with his decision. The sea can be an unforgiving place. She takes no prisoners and we were out in the Atlantic in a force 8 to 9 gale.

For the people not yet sea sick, it was up to the wheel house to ride out the journey back to port. Mark asked if we enjoyed the dive and I could only say that it had been a long awaited dream now fulfilled, thanking him for getting us out there. It was then he told me that only 5 minutes after we dived, the weather just turned and this storm took hold. If we had still been on board, he would have cancelled the dive, so I guess we were bloody lucky. As it was a long journey back, Mark got me to steer his boat back part of the way so he could enjoy a bit of a break. He took the opportunity to call his mate Keith, the skipper of the other boat. I heard Mark tell him all went well, no incidents and two of us got on the wreck. Although Mark wasn't diving and neither was Keith, they were both excited. Keith had given the co ordinates to Mark and talked him in to doing the dive, reassuring him that we were a worthy bunch that would be discreet and stick to the plan. This had been a long old day, but for two of us, well worth it. We were two people that had dived a wreck that only a handful of people had been on. It was a bit like a very exclusive club membership or conquering a mountain climb.

I had to take my hat off to the other divers that gave up a day's diving, so that five of us could go for this. We eventually got in to Stromness at 5 ish and once we had tidied up the boat, it was off to the pub for a celebratory drink. After 20 minutes, a random diver from a different dive boat came over to us and announced he knew we had been on the *Hampshire* today. So much for secrecy. Now everyone in the pub knew. We nodded and then he started on about deep air dives to that depth were foolhardy. Yes, I agreed with him, but pointed out that it depended on the diver in question. He was now back in his place with his mouth shut, heading back to his Trimix buddies. He was just jealous. I knew it, Darren knew it and so did he.

It was Friday the following day and I was happy to just chill out or do whatever anyone else wanted to do. It had been the perfect end to a great week's diving and the memory would stay with me for many years to come.

Good mates

There had been some really funny moments on this holiday and it's true to say that certain people had contributed to it more than others. Darren had quite a dry sense of humour and took no prisoners when an opportunity reared its head. One classic moment still springs to my mind, even after all these years.

Alan was Richard Bull's replacement and had stepped in at the last minute. He was keen as mustard and a first rate diver, but there was help and assistance that you sometimes could do without. For the uninitiated, prior to all dives, a diver must spit in to his mask, rub the inside of the glass and then swill it off with sea or fresh water to stop the glass from misting up when the diver is wearing it. Well, Alan smoked roll ups like they were going out of fashion and he was blessed with no shortage of saliva either. He could probably find enough spit to do all the masks and Darren nick named him the official mask cleaner.

I had just spent 15 minutes kitting up and Darren and I were sat awaiting the call from the skipper to say we were on site and get ready to jump. I called to Alan to pass me my mask. With that, quick as a flash Darren shouted, "Can you spit in Dave's mask and wash it out?" To my horror, he picked it up in an instant and before I could stop him, he had indeed lived up to his name of the official mask cleaner. Darren was in absolute hysterics. I, however, was more reserved and just got him to wash it out well. What was he thinking? I have been diving for 27 years and I have never heard or seen anyone, carrying out this kind of pre dive assistance and I hope I never do. It was funny though, Darren ever the prankster, Alan just wanting to help. With mates like this, you sure didn't need enemies. Crikey, look out, should you ever upset one.

It was Friday and the dives were planned on the block ships. The wreck of the *Tabarka* was lying upside down in just 12 metres of water. She was a 2,624 tonne, single screw steamer. Being upside down there were only a few entry points and so once we were in, these would be our only way out. Once in the water, we quickly made our way down to the hull and located a suitable hole and pulled ourselves in. I turned on my light and the beam cut through the darkness. There were a mass of large boulders that were placed in her, to aid her sinking and keep her from moving once on the bottom. As I finned through the deck, three boilers came in to view and I spent some time exploring them. As I moved over them, I found myself in the engine room with a complete triple expansion engine. It was a great sight as it hung above my head, from the floor, now turned ceiling. The time spent in this wreck had flown by and it was time to retrace our route and locate the exit point. Once outside, we were torn from the wreck as we ascended, but we didn't have any deco to do and just made our way to the surface. What a great little dive.

Later that evening, we had gone to the Royal Hotel for the evening's entertainment, but the weather had turned in and snow was falling. We had got chatting to some local scallop divers we had met earlier in the week. They were a hard working, hard drinking bunch of young guys and their women were even harder. I am not kidding. We had been sat at the bar for about an hour chatting about working as a scallop diver and whether the band would turn up, with the snow now settling on the ground. Buying one another rounds of drinks, it had started with pints but the scallop divers had now upped the ante by introducing chasers.

All of a sudden two of the women started shouting at each other and drinks began to fly. I looked at one of the guys and said "You must earn a good living if your girls can afford to throw good scotch over each other", and it all went silent for a moment. Three things shot through my mind: is there going to be a mass fight at the bar? Will it be just with the girls, guys or both of them? As it happened, with whisky dripping off their face's, the girls began to laugh and just as quick as it all started, it was over. Then, good humoured banter was restored to the high spirited women, the band failed to show and we carried on at the bar, making our own entertainment. At about 2 am, I called it a night and headed back to the boat, hoping that the tide was high and the boat was close to the dock, so I wouldn't risk breaking a limb trying to board her. Leaping from dock to boat, I landed safely, more by luck than judgment, I can tell you.

Saturday morning and all the dive kit had been packed and there was just the 12 hour trip back to Bristol left to do. Although I was not looking forward to it, I had a great time and I was looking forward to my own bed, a big hug from my wife and to see my two boys.

Once back in Bristol, with the *Hampshire* under my belt and a very successful week's diving, I continued to dive 40, 50 and 60 metre wrecks all on air. I must say, my nitrogen narcosis tolerance was at its peak and I wasn't fazed by any depth of dive. The first of these dives was on my old favourite, The *Empress of India*, sat in 46 metres. It was a calm day and as I dropped down the shot line, the visibility was nearly 8 metres. I was using twin 15 litre cylinders with air and 50% and 80% Nitrox mixes for the deco later to come. I finned around the lower part of the wreck and there were rows and rows of brass port holes, 18 inches in diameter, but they were bolted firmly to the hull of this mighty ship and would not be coming off in a hurry. I must have covered quite a bit of this wreck today and after 30 minutes I removed the up line from the back of Darren's cylinders and attached the lift bag to the end of the blue nylon rope. These up lines had been inspired by technical divers in the US and I had got a supplier to build them out of aluminium. They were just a spool, about 2 feet long, with a 6 inch diameter disc at each end to stop the nylon rope coming off. The whole thing would spin, allowing the rope to unwind freely as the lift bag shot to the surface.

With the lift bag attached, I used my spare regulator to put some air in the lift bag and it headed off to the surface, getting faster as the air in the bag expanded the nearer the bag got to the surface. After a minute or two, the line stopped running off the reel and I knew the bag was at the surface. I pulled off a bit extra, tied it off to the wreck and cut the reel free. After stowing the part empty reel back between my buddy's tanks, we were ready to begin our slow ascent. Deco started at 9 metres for 6 minutes, with a further 46 minutes at 6 metres. It was a bit boring, but I had my carton of Ribena with me. After I had settled in to the deco, I put the straw in to the Ribena carton, removed my regulator and took a well deserved drink. The only thing to keep in mind is you have to keep pressure on the carton as you suck out the drink. If you allow the pressure to drop, sea water will be sucked back in to the carton and that would be the end of the drink. I have used this technique quite a few times and have it off to a fine art and for divers who have not witnessed it, it's quite a party piece. If you really want to go the full hog, take out a tube of your favourite Primula spread and chow in to that. I have yet to come up with a suitable cracker to go with it. Water biscuits aren't quite up to it.

Mixed Gas

In late August 1995, I was using Nitrox for most of the dives I was undertaking, but it was costly because most of the mixes were 50 or 80 %. Darren came up with the idea of getting an account with Lyndi Gas, renting some J cylinders and mixing our own in the garage. So, without further ado, the account was in place and we had 3 cylinders in my garage. Two of oxygen and one of helium. We could now mix our own Nitrox or Trimix at a fraction of the cost we would pay at the local dive shop. All we needed to do was decide on the dive depth, boot up the computer and put the info in to the gas programme we were now using.

The gas programme had been acquired from a friend and although it was cutting edge at the time, it was still running on the old DOS system, but it did just what we wanted and was simple to use.

Once all the depths, times and preferred mix had been entered the programme would tell us how much oxygen would need to be decanted in to certain size cylinders, to give a pre determined mix, once they had been topped off with compressed air, giving a 36, 50 or 80 % deco mix or whatever was needed for the particular deco.

When it came to the Trimix fills, it was the same principal, but the helium was put in first, then the oxygen. It was done this way for one simple reason, helium is far more expensive than oxygen and you need more of it than oxygen. When you are decanting a gas from cylinder to cylinder, you are limited by the head pressure in the main J cylinder. Once it drops below what you need in the dive tanks, you need to crack on to a new J cylinder, so after a while, you have various J cylinders with varying pressures in them. In order to use up as much of the gas left in them as possible, we would start filling the dive tanks with the lowest pressure in a particular J cylinder first and then working our way to the next highest and so on, finishing off the fill with a full or near full J cylinder.

The first time I filled my own tanks. I opted for a mix of 17/40, 17% oxygen and 40% nitrogen. The rest was made up of helium, with a 50% and 80% for deco. This was an optimum mix for the diving we were planning to do.

It was 1996 and I was about to get my first taste of the benefits of using Trimix. I was invited to dive a deep wreck called the *Murray*, she lay in the English Channel and was a container ship, sat upright in 60 metres. Darren had dived it before and was raving about it. Although she was a modern ship, the sheer size was something to be seen. Darren had booked a guest house in Torquay and Ian, Darren and I would meet the rest of the divers at the digs. We travelled down together and parked up where we met some of the other divers. They had just arrived too. After a few brief introductions, the owner opened the front door and everyone piled in, like there was some kind of emergency. It was every man for himself, or not as the case may be! Ian and I just followed in behind them, wondering what all the rush was about. Little did we know, we had been had! The owner led Ian and I upstairs and opened the last door. "This is your room lads" he said, pushing open the door and turning away. We walked in and that's when we got the shock of our lives. A double bed! I looked at Ian and he looked at me. I turned back towards the owner, "Hey, this is no good. We need single beds. What are you thinking?", "Oh, I am sorry" he said, this is the only room left. I did say when you booked". That's when we realised why the rest were in a rush to get in and claim their rooms. What would we do without mates?

We put our bags down and looked at the bed. "Well, I am not happy about this" I said, and nor was Ian, but we had paid for the room and the breakfast for two nights. So, with both of us not happy, we took our sides and agreed to sleep one in the bed and the other outside the bed with just a sheet between us. If we had known, we could have brought sleeping bags with us and although it would not have been ideal, it would have been a lot better than this.

We met the rest of the divers downstairs and headed out for some food. On the way there, we were asked how we liked our room. Ha, bloody ha, let's look out for number one, is it? Of course it was. We took a fair bit of leg pulling that weekend I can tell you.

At the pub, 10 of us went to order food. It was just 9 o'clock and the barman said the chef had gone home and there was no hot food. We asked him if he was joking, and no he wasn't. I offered to cook it myself, but he was not having any of it and so 10 hungry men walked out and got fish and chips elsewhere.

Back at the digs, we were trying to get some sleep, but we were both paranoid about the sleeping arrangements and spent most of the night making sure we didn't forget who we were sleeping next to. We did see the funny side in a dark way; our wives would find it very amusing when we told them later. When morning came, we had survived the night. We were down at breakfast by 7 am and out the house and off to the dive boat by 7.45.

Down at the dive boat, the skipper met us and we started loading the dive gear. There were two other divers joining us, one of them was called Nick and he had got a bad skin bend all down his back. It looked like bad sunburn. I felt for him as I had been suffering from skin bends on my shoulders for a while by now and knew how painful they could be just on a small part of the body, but he was not bothered. Darren also pointed out that just last year this guy, along with two other divers, was adrift for three days before being rescued.

He kept himself to himself and after 30 minutes we were loaded and ready to go. The skipper, Johnny Walker, had been taking out divers for many years and was happy taking us out the *Murray*. She is a huge container ship, and Darren, Ian and I were diving as a three. Darren was on Trimix and I was on air with an 80% and 50% for deco. All 4 cylinders were set up across my back and along with that was my up line and battery pack; it weighed a tonne. Nick and his dive buddy had a directional homing device. One half of it stayed with the diver and the other half got attached to the shot line. As one end is pointed in the direction of the other, a series of lights light up as they align with each other. I guess he had no intention of being lost again.

We were ready to dive, the shot line was hooked in to the wreck and I dropped backwards over the side of our dive boat with camera in hand. I swam over to the buoy that was attached to the shot line and made my way down towards the wreck. The water visibility was 15 metres minimum and after a few moments I could see the bridge appearing up through the crystal clear water. We were halfway to France, deep in the English Channel. I would never have expected visibility like this, but here it was. As I landed on the lower part of the bridge at a depth of just over 47 metres, the huge deck area disappeared out in front of me. I located my two buddies and we swam off in the direction of the lower deck. As I descended past 55 metres, I could feel the effects of nitrogen narcosis clouding my head and dulling my senses. Darren turned in front of me and offered me a spare regulator from his Trimix tanks and I inhaled my first breath of this deep diving gas mix. After 3 more breaths, my head cleared and I was fully aware of everything around me. Just as I got used to this new gas, Darren signalled it was time for me to go back on to my air, and just as quickly as my head cleared after 4 breaths with the Trimix, I felt myself slip straight back in to my previous state. At that point, I knew how much of an effect nitrogen narcosis was playing on my deep diving.

Finning around the front of the bridge, I looked up at the T shaped structure that was towering above me. Adding a short burst of air in to my buoyancy jacket, I felt myself ascend towards the bridge windows. I glanced down to check my two buddies were nearby and following my direction. No problem there, they were levelling off at the bridge windows. I stopped and pointed the camera towards the two divers and fired off a few shots. Although the water was clear, the camera had an uncanny ability to capture plankton and any other minute particles that were suspended in the underwater environment, giving your pictures a splattering of what is called back scatter. I would just have to wait and hope that when they got developed, they would be all right.

As I peered through the square windows, there were some other divers inside checking it all out. The captain would have been fighting to save his ship on that same bridge, battling gale force winds, high seas and listing to port with numerous 40 ft containers sliding from her deck in to the sea.

As our dive time drew to an end, we finned back around to the shot line. After checking our dump valves on our suits and buoyancy jackets, all was in good working order. I then located both of my deco valves just to make sure they had not been dislodged or tangled. Double checks prior to an ascent are well worth it. If a dump valve should fail on an ascent, you could race to the surface in a split second, missing all your deco and becoming bent or dead. As for the deco valves, if you can't locate one, then you will be unable to carry out your planned deco stops and you will be in a lot of trouble. So, with all the checks completed, we headed up the shot line to our first stop at 18 metres, then on to further stops at 15, 12, 9 and lastly 6 metres, where we would spend 39 minutes before we finally broke the surface and climbed back aboard the dive boat. I spat out my regulator and found a bench, quickly sitting down so I could take the weight off my back. After a large drink of bottled water, I was helped off with my dive cylinders and I could now catch up with the rest of the divers over a hot cup of tea and discuss the dive. We were all in agreement that it was an awesome dive, even though it was a modern wreck and there were very few artefacts to be found as souvenirs as we liked to call them. Although Ian did manage to get a cup and saucer and I hopefully had some photos. It was a long journey back and it was just about killing time as we passed back through the busy shipping lane to port. We would be back here tomorrow but it wouldn't all go as smoothly as today.

Back at port, we unloaded the empty cylinders. Our skipper was going to fill them back at his place, so we could head off back to our digs, wash, change, and get out to eat. There is one thing about diving; it certainly gives you an appetite. The conversation turned to the dive we were doing tomorrow. It was a wreck called *H M S Formidable*, a 15,250 ton Battleship.

A sequence of events on HMS Formidable

She was a large pre –Dreadnought Battleship launched in 1898 with a water displacement of over 15,000 tons, and she sat in 65 metres of water some 36 miles off the Devon coast. Ironically she was one of the first Battleships to be sunk in the First World War. She was similar in size and armaments to the *Empress of India* but with one difference - she went down in all her glory with guns at the ready.

She was sunk by German submarine *U24* on New year's day 1915 taking two torpedo hits on her port side. Within just two hours, listing and with heavy seas, she sank with the loss of over 551 men. Only 199 were saved and now today she can only be dived by special licence. This was going to be quite a dive in more ways than we yet knew. At 10.30 pm we were heading back to our digs. It was an early start and I for one was tired out.

We were up at 6am and our landlady had cooked our breakfast. We quickly devoured them, but they were a bit on the small size and Darren was not very pleased about it. As he left the B&B, he wrote his comments in the comments book. We loaded our belongings in to our cars and headed off to the dive boat. The skipper was waiting for us and once the dive gear was aboard, we pushed off. It was about 4 to 5 hours to the dive site and the weather was looking changeable, with the prospect of a strengthening wind towards the afternoon.

We would be diving in a three again and Ian would be diving with just twin 12 litre cylinders, the same as he used the previous day on the *Murray*. I would be using my trusty twin 15 litre cylinders along with twin 7 litre cylinders filled with 50% and 80% oxygen for deco. Darren had the same set up as me, but was using twin 12 litre cylinders with a weak Trimix fill, left over from the dive yesterday. This he had achieved by getting his cylinders re filled with just compressed air, but it would do the job for the dive ahead.

We checked over our dive kit and all was working fine, so all we could do was drink tea and rest up until we got to the dive site. The skipper was sat in the wheel house of the converted pot fishing boat with his book, feet up and with a mug of tea in his hand. Not a bad way of making a living, I was thinking. There were 5 of us in the wheel house chatting and looking out at the various ships that were steaming to and from their destinations. In the shipping lane, I had spotted a large container ship similar to the one we had dived yesterday. It was heading in our direction and getting closer. The skipper still had his nose in the book he was reading and we all took it as read that he was aware of the ship to our starboard side; it was big enough not to be missed. It was getting bigger as it closed in on us. I shot a glance to Darren, as if to say "Has he seen it? Hell, it's a bit close, it's very close!" Someone, I can't remember who, shouted "Hey John, are we meant to be this close to…." and before he could finish the sentence, John was on his feet, spinning the wheel to port. We passed this massive ship with just a few feet between us. Our boat was wooden and was dwarfed by the ship. If it had collided with us, we would have sunk and the ship would have probably been unaware it had even hit us. John looked at us all and just said "That was close. And by the way, if you ever see something you don't think I am aware of, please let me know". Sure thing, John.

Looking up at the bridge of the Giannis D 35 meters below the surface

Below a section of the deck

A leisurely dive on one of Egypt's reefs

Below just emerging through the funnel of the Giannis D after making my way up through the wreck

Fining along the deck of the Giannis D now listing at 45 degrees

Below heavy machinery just waiting to be put in to action

Fining along the wreck of the Zenobia

Below the dive crew on the rusting deck of the block ship Inverlane

Dave Blackmore scaling the ladder from hell on Brian Charles boat just off the coast of Weymouth on a hot day in August, in full dive kit.

Below Dawn, Ian, and Darren on a cold winters morning in Oban with Poo woods behind them.

The MV Sunrise battling through the rough seas of Scapa Flow to pick us up

Below The silent wreck of the block ship Inverlane

Spoils from the Duke of Buccleuch: Above ornate glass wear

Hand painted plates and bowls below. Two shell cases and WW II Shaving kits.

The rocky decent we made on our way to the 79 meter dive in Malta.

Early days diving on the wreck of the Empress of India off the boat MV Grace 15 miles out and hardly a ripple on the water.

Below Darren and Myself under the deck of The Sunrise suited and booted; ready to dive

My first ever open water dive down at Hope Cove left to right me two girls from the pub Bill and Alan who made his own wet suit!

Below Me and the Dutch girl on a night dive in Malta and not a Shark in sight.

Dave Blackmore and Darren Woodward just about to step of the MV Sunrise for a dive on the wreck of the battleship Markgraf.

Below my new dive buddies in the lime stone walls of Blue Springs, Florida

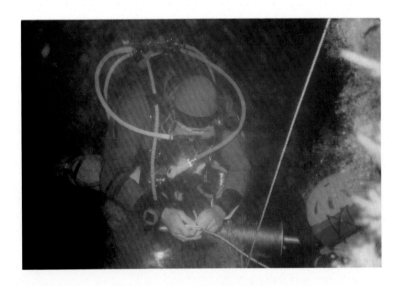

Securing the up line at 57 meteres on the wreck of The Boadicea

Below Me and Andy Mawditt kitting up to dive the wreck of the Empress of India.

Darren and me in quiet contemplation on our way to dive the Wreck of the Hampshire.

Below just surfaced from the 80 meter dive in Malta

Looking up as I make my way out of Blue Springs Florida

Below me and my Brother Mike in our early days on Roger's hard boat just about to dive a wreck out of Swanage

Posing by the mine DR John Derek and me

Darren and me making for the shot line leading down to the Hampshire

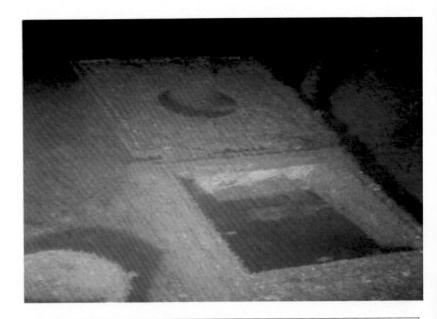

An inviting hatchway on the James Barrie

Early days at Scapa Flow under the sheltered deck of the Sunrise L T R Dave, Alex, Darren, and me

The good ship MV Sunrise it was the best live a board back in the 80 s and still is in 2009

Above the dive crew on the propeller of the Hampshire

And far below a tranquil dive on the Carnatiic, forever stranded on Sha'Abu Nuhas Reef

A bit of tunnel vision through the remains of the wreck of the Carnetic

Resting within the lime scale walls of Blue Springs Florida.

Looking through the remaining structure of the Carnetic

Below light beaming through the window to the surface from the depths of the Giannis D

Breaking out from the depths of the Carnetic, the tunnel to the open sea

Below the striking silhouette of the block ship Inverlane rising from the depths

Struggling up the Sunrise ladder

Remaining structure of the Carnatic Below

Typical technical dive; at ease decompressing on the deco line

Drifting through the Carnatic. This is what diving is all about.

Relaxing in the sun; Scapa Flow 2009

With this near miss behind us, or should I say alongside us, we pushed on at a steady pace through an ever increasing swell towards the wreck of the *Formidable*. John let us know we were just under an hour away and we started to kit up on the open deck of the fishing boat. As luck would have it, there was plenty of space and I could pick my preferred spot to get ready. Ian and Darren did the same. It had been agreed that we would be hitting the water first and that suited me. With the sea swell as it was, after a 5 hour steam out there, the last thing I wanted was a bout of sea sickness.

I was nearly ready to dive. My twin 15 litre main tanks were pumped to 250 bar and either side of these were my 7 litre deco tanks, one filled with 50% and one with 80% Nitrox. These would speed up my decompression penalties on my return to the surface, and at that depth, there would be quite a lot. The dive plan was to spend a maximum 20 minutes on the bottom and then to send up our own deco line to the surface and use it to carry out a safe, controlled ascent to the surface. Great plan, but as they say, shit happens. The skipper was hooked in to the wreck and we three were ready to dive. With a slight lean backwards, I was over the side and in the water. Darren and Ian were swimming towards the shot line and I followed closely behind them. In this swell, if anyone of us missed the shot line as the current sped us towards the buoy line, it would mean that the boat would have to come around and pick up the diver, get them back on board and start all over again. This could take up to 10 minutes, resulting in that diver being stressed and lower on air than the original dive plan had been based on, but we were professionals and we grabbed the shot line. With a quick check, we headed down the shot line.

The visibility was a good 15 metres or more. At 40 metres down, it was getting very dark, even though the water was clear. I switched on my dive light and 50 watts of power lit up the blackness in front of me.

At 50 metres, I started to recognise a large dark shadow beneath me. The shot line looked like it was leading all the way to the sea bed alongside the wreck. I could taste the metallic taste of the air I was breathing through my regulator and heard the loud sound of my exhaust bubbles as they were expelled in to the abyss. Compressed air at depth has a taste to it and to say its pleasant would be a lie, but you breathe it down just the same. If I were on Trimix, I wouldn't be experiencing this. My only consolation is that both Darren and Ian were dealing with the same.

Slowing my descent as I touched bottom at 65 metres, I put some more air both in to my suit and buoyancy jacket adjusting it until I was neutrally buoyant. My two buddies did the same. After checking gauges, we finned off down one side of the wreck. Darren had his lights on and between us we had over a 150 watts of light, but it was still black as night down there. We picked up on a large gun running out across the sand. Unlike her sister, this wreck was not decommissioned prior to her sinking. A few feet further away from the first gun, I spotted its companion. These guns were massive; just what you would expect from a battleship of 15,000 tonnes. Darren was leading the dive up in to a large piece of superstructure, it's twisted, unrecognisable shape was over 6 inches thick in places and it was even darker on this part of the wreck. We decided to drop back over to the other side of the wreck and finned along the length of it. Ian was just a few feet from the sea bed and Darren and I were above him at about 58 metres. Checking my dive timer, we had been down for just over 18 minutes and it was time to go. After a few moments we got Ian's attention and he got the picture. I removed Darren's up line reel from between his main tanks and we attached a lift bag to the end of the blue nylon line.

With the bag secured, I used my spare regulator to put some air in the bag. I pressed the purge button on my Poseidon regulator and a mass of bubbles escaped in to the yellow lift bag and it began to rise. Darren held both ends of the reel as we watched the nylon rope disappear from the spool, getting faster and faster as the air in the bag expanded as it got closer to the surface. After about a minute or so, it stopped and we tied it off to the wreck before cutting the line from the spool. I quickly stowed the reel back behind the tanks again and we were ready to leave the wreck and start our controlled ascent. Ian was relying on his dive computer for the various decompression stops. Darren and I had pre determined stops that we had written down on a slate that was attached to our dive timers. Our first stop was at 25 metres, but there was a problem. The lift bag that was attached to our up line was sinking back down towards us. Shit, we didn't need this. I could see Ian just below the bag and couldn't understand why he had not noticed that the bag needed more air putting in it and that it was sinking. Darren got a smaller lift bag out and we struggled to attach it to the sinking up line. This was all taking time. We should have been at 25 metres, but we had been forced to come up to 18 metres to sort the situation out. All the time I was thinking "What's with Ian?" Why couldn't he have just put some air in the bloody bag? I guessed Darren had the same thoughts.

After 5 minutes, with the extra bag secured, we were stable and back in control at 18 metres. We had missed the 3 minute stop at 25 metres whilst deploying the second lift bag. I switched over to my first deco mix and looked at Darren. We had over 1 hour of deco to do and the start of it had been less than perfect. The current was begging to run and looking up we could see the lift bag beginning to sink again. This was not good. If the lift bag was not on the surface, the dive boat would not know that we were safe doing our deco. Also, we would be unable to carry out our deco properly. We needed to fix this situation and fast. Signalling to Ian who was hanging under the lift bag that was now horizontal at 10 metres below the surface, we got no positive response to the rapidly deteriorating situation. I finished my 3 minutes deco stop at 18 metres and headed up the line to see what the hell was going on with Ian and the bloody lift bag.

I reached Ian, hanging on just under the bag. I took my main regulator and shot a large burst of air in to the bag and sent it upwards to the surface. There, I thought, why didn't you do that? I signalled to Ian to express my displeasure at his lack of response. You may ask how you make yourself understood underwater with no communication available; well, you improvise. I lifted both my arms in to the water between us and he got my drift. He showed me his computer. I had never seen such deco time in my life. There was over 3 hours on the display. Then he showed me both his contents gauges. He had 20 bar in one and less than 20 bar in the other. To say he was screwed would be an understatement and I could see the concern on his face. I showed him my two gauges for my now redundant 15 litre cylinders. There was over 100 bar in each. I didn't need the air left in them as I was now using both my 7 litre deco cylinders. He seemed to be a bit more reassured after seeing that. I showed him 20 on my hands and dropped back down to Darren, who had by now got a white slate out and a pencil. I took it from him and wrote down the situation. Above 3 hours deco, less than 40 bar of air left, he could breathe my air once we got up to him. We would then need to come up with an exit plan for him and fast.

We continued our deco stops at 12 metres, 9 metres and finally 6 metres. I then changed over to my 80% deco mix and handed Ian one of my main tank regulators. My deco would be finished in 25 minutes. Darren would be finished a little bit sooner. We had more than enough air to keep Ian out of trouble for now, but he couldn't stay in the water for 3 hours, and we certainly didn't have sufficient spare air in all our tanks to cover it. We would need help from above in the form of oxygen.

As Darren finished his deco some minutes earlier than me, it was down to him to get the plan in to action. Within seven minutes, a diver was in the water and he was carrying a spare tank with an 80% Nitrox mix. This would speed up his decompression and get him out of the water in time for tea. I had now finished my deco and left Ian with his new friend, the 80% deco cylinder and headed up to the surface. As my head popped up out of the waves, I could see the boat just a few metres away. It was good to see the sunlight and feel the fresh sea air on my face. I finned over to the boat and grabbed hold of the ladder and began to climb up the rungs. As my upper body came out of the water I could feel the weight of all my dive equipment on my legs; it was a rude awakening after being suspended weight free for nearly 80 minutes. I felt the weight on my legs ease and I looked up to see a fellow diver had hold of my tanks and was pulling me up the remainder of the ladder. As I reached the top of the ladder, I was able to step in to the boat and plonk my tired ass down on to a bench seat and get the 4 tanks off my back and have a well deserved cup of tea.

Darren brought me over a mug of tea and a few of the other divers came over to get an update on what had happened. As in most cases, it was a sequence of events and a lack of attention. If Ian had been monitoring his computer and air, he would have seen the deco racking up and his air diminishing, long before it reached the problem stage. After 40 minutes, Ian emerged and was soon back on board the boat, looking rather sheepish. We put him on a further 80% mix and sat him down as a precaution. We were all very relieved and I guess Ian was too.

I took off my suit and noticed that both my shoulders were red hot; you could have fried an egg on them. I could have done without this. I had not missed any deco as such and had used a 10% safety factor in my dive plan, but I had had these symptoms before. The other divers came over to have a look and take the mick. One of them reckoned I could get a bend sitting on wet grass. Nice one, Paul. It was not quite that bad, well, that was what I kept telling myself.

With all the divers back on board, John the skipper, broke the news that due to the sea swell we wouldn't be able to return to the port we set off from and that we would need to go back to Brixham. The problem was our van. Ian's van was back where we set off from and John would have to ferry Ian and a few others back to get their vehicles. The round trip would be a good few hours and so we headed on back to Brixham with the sea swell, making our way back a long and slow affair. It was dusk as we reached the shelter of Brixham and John took the drivers back to get the vehicles. The rest of us had to go to the pub and wait for them to return; life is tough sometimes, we told ourselves but someone has to do it.

Down on the boat, the tide had gone out and we had to tie all the equipment to a rope and pull it up to the top of the dock. With the van loaded, we set off. Ian put his foot down and Darren and I fell asleep. I did open my eyes at some point and we seemed to be speeding through the night at break neck speed. Rather than worry about 'what if something comes the other way?' I swiftly went back to sleep. We were back in Bristol within an hour and a half; that was some driving in a fully loaded Transit van, I can tell you.

Less than a month later, I was booked on a dive to visit the wreck of the *Boadicea* sat in 57 metres with a dive duration of 92 minutes.

Diving officer Portway diving club 1996

I was now in a new dive club called Portway Divers. They were about one mile from the Bristol suspension bridge. They met up on a Thursday night and had about 40 members, although not all of the members were divers.

The club was founded in the seventies as just a swimming club and progressed in to a diving club in the early 70s. Having been approached by the then acting diving officer for the club, I soon took over the role when he stood down at the next AGM. Little did I know what I had let myself in for. There were a few strong characters in the club and we would lock horns at some point, I just didn't think it would be so soon.

Just one week after being nominated and voted in as Dive Officer, I was approached by the training officer, who made it crystal clear to me that she had her doubts whether she could work with me. Slightly taken aback, I engaged her on the matter where she pointed out that she would do things her way or not at all. Now, I am all for being committed and focussed, but this is a club, not a kinder garten or multi million pound company. I gave her the benefit of the doubt and reassured her I would do my best to leave her to it and wandered over to the bar for a pint; end of round one.

The club house was a ram shackle, wooden, pre fabricated type building, but the people were friendly and as clubs go, most members mixed in well and had a live and let live attitude.

We had some new trainees join up and they were progressing through their training and with all things said and done, the instructor was a very accomplished diver and a very competent instructor. Putting the trainees through their paces all was well, until I got a phone call one Sunday evening from one of the trainees.

She began by enlightening me on how she and two other trainees had gone off on their own and dived some dive site and some things had happened. One of them had got separated and it was deep and dark and she had run out of air. She had been forced to make a buoyant ascent, where on the surface; she was picked up and whisked off to the decompression chamber at Plymouth. Not to worry, she was all right and so were the other two divers, oh well, I thought, that makes it all OK then, NOT.

As the Dive Officer, I needed to be told about all dives that were going on and although this was not necessarily a club dive, they were not qualified divers and were still progressing through their training. There was nothing stopping anyone with a handful of cash buying a set of diving equipment and jumping off the nearest pier and killing themselves, but not on my watch.

As the DO and the Training Officer, we would be likely to attend an inquest if one or two of our members were to lose their lives and we could all do without that. As I mentioned before, it's just a sport and key people are there to train and guide new members, not to parent them, but rules had been bent and common sense had not prevailed. They obviously knew that if we had been made aware of their plans, we would have talked it over with them and pointed out that they weren't ready for this level of diving. As every experienced diver knows, diving in a three is not the best way to dive; pairs are best, as you can keep an eye on each other far more easily.

But they had told no one, for this or perhaps some other reason, and the incident had occurred. Their instructor had been told prior to the call made to me. After about an hour of listening to the ins and outs and the ifs, mights and maybes, I ended the call with thoughts on the inevitable debrief on the whole episode.

The Instructor called me later that evening, not very pleased and was keen to tackle the three of them on Thursday. With that to look forward to, I hung up and reflected on what was left of my Sunday night and the implications of the meeting now planned for Thursday night. One thing was for certain, there would be some winners and some losers. Well, I couldn't wait; who the Hell wants an easy life.

We met at the club and used a quiet, spare room to discuss the events that led to an unqualified diver ending up in the deco chamber, and why the three of them had just gone off and put themselves in that position. As with most non fatal incidents that happen within a club, trying to extract the truth and reasoning behind things was somewhat a waste of time. However, the trainer put some restrictions in place. The men were not to embark on taking under qualified members out without prior consultation with either herself or me and the girl would be limited to a maximum depth of 10 metres for the next 4 dives, just to be sure there would be no more buoyant ascents or poor air management. Everyone seemed to be OK with this and that was that, or so I thought.

I had put together a trip up to Scapa Flow for early April next year and it was important that all 3 of them finished their training and that the trainee proved herself in the water. The two guys were fine, but although she was OK in the water, there was a personality clash with her trainer and no matter what she did, it wasn't good enough. I had observed her diving and could see nothing wrong with it. She had been taught very well by her trainer, but they could not get on, and after 6 weeks of the 10 metre restriction, I had a quiet word with the trainer and suggested that she pass the end of her training over to one of our other instructors. That was that, she resigned from the club and was never seen at the club again. The club lost a valued member and instructor. The trainee got a new instructor and finished her training. I leave it to your thoughts as to who lost and who won. All is fair in love and war. Clubs and members are no different and in early April 1997 we would all be together again, one big happy family aboard the good ship *Sunrise*, oh I can hardly wait.

In late October 1996, I was diving the wreck of the *HMS Boadicea*, sat upright in 57 metres of water off Portland Bill. She was a B class Destroyer sunk on the 13 June 1944 by German aircraft. Heading down the shot line, the visibility was 10 metres plus and landing on the deck, I soon recognised the rows of depth charges still in situ ready to roll off the deck in to action. They were much bigger than I thought they would have been, but then again, I had only seen them on old films. These ones were about the size of a 45 gallon oil drum. Finning over the top of them, I gave them a wide berth, and a thought flowed through my mind "If one of these went off, it would be goodnight for all 12 divers in the water" and with that, I continued towards the bow. The wreck itself was clearly recognisable large sections could be identified and as we reached where the stern should be it was clearly gone - blown off by the bombs that sank her. All too soon, we had spent 30 minutes on her and it was time to start our deco run to the surface. I helped Paul send the up line to the surface and tie it in to the wreck. We were on our way without a hitch, unlike the time Darren, Ian and I spent on the Formidable up line. This one went like clockwork. Just as well as we had 60 minutes of deco to do and various gas changes. It had been a great dive. Paul, as I remember, discovered his drysuit was not so dry after 10 minutes in to the first deco stop, but there was nothing either of us could do, so he just had to put up with it. What a trooper. I didn't hear him moan once. Something to do with the regulator that was stuck in his mouth for the duration. He moaned plenty back on the boat though. Well, nobody is perfect, hey.

I took plenty of photos that day and passed the time on the shot line drinking Ribena from a carton I had taken with me on the dive. It's a good way of getting a well needed drink on these long deco stops.

The following week, I was back diving with Paul Gibson on an unknown wreck again off Portland Bill in 57 metres, with a dive plan of 92 minutes; 30 minutes on the wreck and 62 minutes deco. Again, the visibility was unbelievable with over 15 metres of clear water in every direction. With visibility this good any wreck is worth diving and as I recall this one was on the money for both Paul and myself.

Back at the surface, with all deco stops carried out to the book, both my shoulders were playing up and the skin bends had hit again with a vengeance; this could seriously effect my diving ability in the near feature .

It took days for my shoulders to get back to normal and I would have to try and come up with a solution to this problem. I finished the dive season of 1996 and packed away my kit ready for 1997 and the forth coming trip back up to Scapa Flow in early April.

Portway divers at Scapa Flow 1997

My time spent as Dive Officer was also very amusing. Just after the saga of the girl in the deco chamber running out of air and missing her stops, I took 11 divers from the club up to Scapa Flow. The fab four were among the 11 and emotions were still raw to say the least, but we had all paid up, and no one was keen on backing down or out of the trip. 'Hell, I am going to do it anyway' was their mind set, and that's what I liked about people who had a point or an axe to grind in the club.

As the new Dive Officer at Portway Divers, I had organised yet another trip to Scapa Flow. Once I had announced the plan, the other 11 places were filled within two weeks and all deposits were paid up. The trusty *MV Sunrise* was booked for the beginning of April.

All the divers were from the dive club, including the fab four from the previous saga all happily reunited, but they would not all be diving together and that would be the secret to a successful diving holiday aboard the confines of a small boat. Even back in the day, you had to do a risk assessment, or was it just common sense?!

As it was very early in the year, the weather would be challenging and we would need to be prepared for anything Mother Nature could throw at us. Half of us decided to use argon gas for suit inflation. This was achieved by bringing a J cylinder with us and decanting it in to small 3 litre cylinders, just for our suit inflation.

I also brought with me lots of thick, warm clothes and a substantial under suit. We all arranged our own travel up to Thurso and would meet up at a Travel Inn type of place for the evening prior to the sailing across to Stromness.

Our ferry crossing wasn't until noon so we didn't have to get up too early. After checking out, we parked up and unloaded the kit in to one of the big containers that were used to transport divers kit across to Stromness and then boarded the ferry just in time for dinner; we docked at 2 pm and went to find the *Sunrise* and the skipper, Mark.

He met me with a firm hand shake as I stepped aboard. The sun was shining and the boat had just been painted, ready for the new dive season. After a few introductory pleasantries, the whole gang were all settled in. Bunks had been chosen and preferred seats in the saloon had been occupied. This was by far the best boat up here in Stromness and everyone was happy with her.

Mark gathered us all in the saloon, to tell those of us that had not been aboard before, how the water, electric and toilets worked. He then set out the week's dive plan. As there were over 10 charter boats operating and only 9 major wrecks in the Flow, he and the other skippers would try and work it so that only one boat would be on any particular wreck at any one time. That way, we would get the best chance at good visibility on the wrecks.

The first dive was on the Sunday and a shallow cruiser had been selected. At 8.30 am, we were all kitting up under the false metal roof of the *Sunrise* that covered the whole of the bow section of the deck. Although I had kitted up under this roof dozens and dozens of times, I still managed to hit my head on it from time to time, and so did everyone else who was over five feet five. Boy, did you know it. The roof was unforgiving and after the first encounter, you made damn sure to avoid any further contact with it, but it did offer great dry protection from the wind and rain that was now battering us.

The first pair of divers got ready, jumped over the side in to the water and made their way to the buoy. After a few checks, they disappeared beneath the now heavy sea swell. The wind was blowing hard and the rain was lashing down as we came round for the second drop off. One of the two divers realised he did not have his weight belt on and there were a few minutes delay before he was ready. Mark had to do a new run, so that they were jumping up current from the buoy and would drift down onto it. The whistle blew and over they went. Darren and I stood up and waited for the next run. The swell was not improving and as we neared the drop off point, the sea came right up high, level with the deck at the exit point and I stepped off. I gently got immersed in the dark swell as it carried me to the buoy. Then, as the swell fell away, the *Sunrise* disappeared from view. Darren was at my side and after a quick check, we dropped down the shot line to the serenity and calm of the depths, leaving behind the turbulent waters above.

I closed my dump valve on my shoulder, turned on my 50 watt underwater light and continued down the shot line towards the wreck. Although the water was dark from the lack of sunlight, it was clear, with a visibility of a least 10 metres. Touching down on the wreck, I put some more argon in to my suit to equalise the pressure, then set off to explore the wreck. Large sections were clearly visible and we had a good first dive. Leaving the wreck, we made our way up the shot line, completed our stops and surfaced.

We bobbed in the heavy swell. One minute I could see the boat, the next she was gone. This would be fun climbing back up the ladder. As I grabbed it, I began hauling myself up, rung by rung. Reaching the top, I crawled on my hands and knees across the pitching deck and back to my bench seat, where help was at hand to get me out of my kit.

With all back on board, we ate breakfast and discussed the dive and the plan for the next dive in the afternoon. It was clear to us that with the weather conditions and amount of kit we were using, it would be necessary for a staggered dive plan, so that dive preparations could be assisted by two divers that would dive last, once everyone else was in the water. We put this in to practice in the afternoon and it worked well.

The next day, Karen and Steve helped with the first dive as we would all do at some point during the week. We all had a much more relaxed start to the dive, even with the wind and sea swell still making diving conditions difficult. Darren and I were the first in the water and like the day before, the visibility was good. Once on the wreck of the *Dresden*, we finned off along the sea bed with the wreck to our right, entering some large holes and various hatches. After 10 minutes, I made my way to the stern and continued along the side of this silent wreck. Reaching the shot line at the bow, we checked our gauges and headed up to carry out our deco. Again, back on the surface while we waited to be picked up, I took the opportunity to fire off some photos of the *Sunrise* as she approached us through the swell. Our skipper had positioned the boat between us and the gusting winds. We climbed the ladder and got back on to the deck in relative comfort, but it was still a killer on the old legs going up the ladder with four cylinders on your back. Rich Barrett was there with his camera to capture the moment when I panted like a dog on my hands and knees whilst I caught my breath back on the pitching deck.

It was mid week and the dive for the morning was the wreck of the trawler the *James Barry*. She had been down only a few years, sat in 45 odd metres, just outside the flow and could only be dived at slack water. We would all have to be kitted up and in the water as one. As luck would have it, the sun was out and the wind had dropped dramatically. This was a big change from the last few days, but very welcome. At 7 am, the engine started up and we were off. I had a light breakfast of toast and tea and set about checking my kit; we would be diving in 40 minutes.

With 20 minutes to go, we all began to kit up and with a bit of help from the skippers mate and two non divers, we were all ready with 5 minutes to spare. Mark gave the word and we all went over the side like lemmings. I took hold of the shot line and descended down the orange nylon line towards the wreck of the *James Barry*. The water was gin clear and I could see the wreck at less than 30 metres, sat upright on the bottom. It looked like a toy boat. After a further few minutes, I let go of the shot line and finned off towards her. I fired off some shots from my camera and managed to get round the whole of the wreck before it was time to get back to the shot line. The rudder and prop were still on her and there were hatches and windows to explore. We headed back to the shot line and started our decompression. As I ascended the line, I could feel the current pulling me from the line and at 6 metres I had ten minutes of deco to do. The current was even stronger and the orange line was so slippery we all found ourselves sliding up it, no matter how hard we gripped it. We all had to shimmy down the line every minute or so, just to remain at 6 metres. This in turn made the initial 10 minutes deco take nearly 20. With the constant up and down antics and with every minute the current getting stronger, we were like flags in a gale. It was a great dive though and worth every minute. I checked my computer; I was clear and was relieved to reach the surface. I signalled to the boat and let go of the buoy. Within 30 seconds, I was 50 or so metres from the buoy. That gave an indication of how fast the tide was now running.

Mark, being the excellent skipper he was, soon had us located and back on board the *Sunrise*. Once I had got out of my dive gear, I headed down to the saloon for a well deserved breakfast. After finishing my breakfast, Mark asked me to steer the boat in the direction of our next dive location. I must admit, it was a pleasure and although she was a big old girl with an old gardener engine, she handled well and I was only too happy to have the helm for 40 minutes, whilst Mark filled the dive cylinders for the afternoon dive. He was a past master at multi tasking and with oxygen whips and high pressure compressor hoses; he soon had all the tanks filled and was back in the wheel house to check my boat handling skills. Well, I hadn't hit anything and we were still on course, so I guess I did all right. It would have been a different story back in the confines of the port, we would have probably been diving a new wreck called the *Sunrise*.

Between dives we stopped off at various locations and even if it was the main town of Stromness, there was not a great deal to do. Some years ago, Darren and I were up there diving and we discovered a bar down some steps and nick named it Huggy Bear's Den, after the Starski and Hutch series. It was a dingy place and apart from two girls in there, it was empty. These two looked like a Dick Emery sketch, one was about four feet something and the other one looked like Dick Emery in drag; we left pretty smartly.

That was years ago and we had regaled the story to some of the guys on this trip. One afternoon, half of us went in search of the legendry Huggy Bear Club and the two characters that had occupied the doorway all those years ago. After a few false turns and locked doors, by heck, there we were and so were the two women, just how we had described them. Dick Emery and her stunt midget. We were in fits of laughter and these two must have thought us mad or very rude. We had a drink and moved on back to the boat. On the way back, the lads were gob smacked. They had thought we had made the place up along with the two characters; well that passed a few hours between dives.

The afternoon dive would be on the *Karlsruhe,* a light cruiser lying in 24 metres of water. At its shallow depth, we should have a good long dive on her. Dropping down the shot line, the visibility was nearly 15 metres and I was planning to do some wreck penetration. Darren and I entered a large open hatch and clipping on my reel we finned deeper in to the wreck. As I took a quick look back to check the exit point, it was still visible, even though we had both finned inside. Over 20 metres, the water was still clear and the exit lit with sunlight from the surface. Continuing in further, we located the spare anchor and chain in a small room. What a find! We had a quick look around and with nothing else to see in this room, we headed back out of the wreck, the way we came. Outside of the wreck, I checked my air and dive time. I still had a good 12 minutes left to dive and my buddy signalled he wanted to check out the port side of the stern. I signalled OK and we went our separate ways for 5 minutes. He finned off to my left, he was only 10 metres away and I carried on exploring on my own for 5 minutes. I spotted a large, long tear hole. I was completely horizontal as I dropped through it and in to the small room. After a few minutes, I decided there was nothing of interest and decided to exit the room the way I had come in, but to my surprise, my cylinders hit the top of the opening. I tried again and the cylinders clanged against the steel again. I tried once more and this time I tried to pull myself out using my hands. The cylinders jammed and I was now stuck half in and half out. I could see the other divers not far away, but they couldn't see me.

I could feel the wreck gripping me and my heart started to pound. I talked myself calm and my breathing rate slowed to near normal. I waved an arm in the direction of the other divers, but they still didn't see me. I had now been in this hole for five minutes. It seemed like a lot longer, but one thing was crystal clear, I hadn't got all day to mess around down here. With a lot of pushing and wriggling, I freed myself from the grip of the lonely ship wreck, but I was still inside it. I checked my air, 100 bar in one and 50 in the other. I needed to think this situation out and fast. I had tried finning straight out, but at the angle I was at, my cylinders just got stuck. I could take them off and push them out first, but the room was quite small and I didn't fancy getting in a tangle and discarded that idea. Then I had it; I lay horizontal and floated out sideways, just as I had come in, and to my relief, I was out. I checked my air and headed for the shot line. As I reached it, I switched to my other tank. That had been a close shave. You just never know when something as simple as dropping in to a wreck is going to create a situation like that. It's a cold reminder to never get complacent, even if the water is gin clear and the depth is only 20 metres. Shit can happen, you have just got to keep your head, once panic sets in, you're finished. I was sure glad I had my twin 12 litre tanks with me that day.

Back on the surface, I told Darren about it and he said that he had assumed I had just finished my dive and gone to the surface on my own. I guess a valuable lesson was learnt that afternoon, certainly by me, and now it was time for a cup of tea and a slice of cake!!

I was in the galley and as it was someone's birthday one of the divers had kindly donated a sponge cake, and it just needed a jam and cream filling to top it off. I had a small pot of whipping cream, but no whisk. No problem, I thought, I can just shake it until its thick! So, after 5 minutes of shaking, the lid came off and semi whipped cream hit every side and appliance in the galley. Karen had just stepped in to the galley doorway and with one quick glance at me burst out laughing as the cream dripped from every possible surface including me. I never knew there was so much cream in a small pot. The under suit I was wearing stank of soured milk within 2 days. What a bloody mess! It took me two hours to clean up the galley and I bet it smelt long after we had gone home, as did my under suit.

In the evening, we headed off to Burray for a meal together, some well deserved drinks and a chill out around the pool table. That is the one time I tend to play pool, and it shows. I wouldn't make it as a hustler, that's for sure. Some of the other guys were quite good and got to stay on the table for hours.

Back on the boat, it was time for bed and I was ready for it. Tomorrow we would be diving the block ships and Rich Barrett was taking his video camera, hoping to get some good footage. We all wanted to be on it, so I had better get my beauty sleep along with the rest of the dive crew.

In the morning we woke to bright sunshine and a flat sea. Great, summer had come early and it was only April, but it wouldn't last. After breakfast, we headed out and the sky had dark clouds gathering on the horizon. Once on the wreck, we all got kitted up and in to the water. The visibility was 20 metres and Rich had his camera to hand, but there was a small problem of a misted up lens. He carried on filming anyway and we all took it in turns getting in front of the lens.

Breaking open a sea urchin, a large wrasse came in to feed, ripping out the centre of the shell. I kept my fingers well out of the mouth of the fish as they could inflict a bite. They got fed regularly by divers and followed me round as I made my way around the wreck. As the tide started to run, I headed back to the surface, only to find the weather had blown up and the sea was now quite choppy.

As we pulled in to Stromness at the end of the day, snow and high winds had created a blizzard and we had to drive 700 miles home in the morning. So much for summer, only 8 hours ago. There was only one thing to do, find a pub, get something to eat and sit out the storm to see what the morning would bring.

The evening was long and the storm raged on in to the night. We shared some beers and chatted about the week's diving well in to the night, tired and happy we headed back to the boat which now had a good covering of snow. We carefully climbed aboard and hit our bunks until the morning. At 6 am, we unloaded all our kit and stowed it in a container ready for the crossing.

Back in Bristol, I continued to play an active part as DO in Portway Divers, organising and participating in various dives and joining other people's expeditions.

The wreck of the Zenobia

It was August 1997, I and the family were off to Cyprus and I was hoping to grab a dive on the wreck of the *Zenobia*.

The wreck of the *Zenobia* is listed as one of the top ten wrecks to dive, certainly in the Med. She was built in 1979, in Malmo, Sweden and was 560 feet long, 75 feet wide and weighed 120,000 tonnes. Powered by two 7 cylinder 2 stroke engines, producing over 18700 bhp, she could achieve over 21 knots, but only spent 34 days in service before she sank. After leaving Sweden, she entered the Med through the Gibraltar Strait and was listing to port. After 4 days in Pireaus, the water was pumped out and on the 3rd June 1980, she continued on to Larnaca where she was again listing to port. After engineers inspected the ship, it was discovered that the complex ballast system was still pumping sea water in to the listing side. The Captain sent the engineers back to port and the ship was anchored just off the coast of Larnaca, where on the 7th June 1980, she sank in 42 metres of water. Over £200 million worth of trucks and cargo were lost, and today over 100 trucks are still on her.

It was a family holiday and I would keep the diving to a minimum. With two young children to keep amused, it would be a full time job and so it was all about quality not quantity. The weather was hot and even the breeze was burning unprotected skin. Leaving the cool, air-conditioned bar, I walked up the road to the dive shop to see what was on offer. It was a typical PADI dive school and they were very laid back. After a few introductory words, they told me I could dive with them the next day on the wreck of the *Zenobia*. I arranged to meet them at the shop as I had no transport and the boat was set to depart some miles further down the resort. 'OK then; see you at 8 am' and that was that.

Back at the bar I told Kay all about the pending dive. I had heard plenty about this wreck over the years, but had never dived it before and was looking forward to diving her.

The next day I grabbed my dive bag and set off up the road to the shop. It had just turned 7.30 am and the shop was still shut. I waited 15 minutes and lo and behold, the man from the shop turned up to collect some cylinders and looked at me with some surprise. "That's OK" I said, "I am meant to be diving with you today". "Crikey, you are lucky. We had forgotten about you and had only dropped by the shop to pick up some dive kit. If you had been 5 minutes later, we would have missed you". Oh great, I thought. Best keep my wits about me, just in case they forget me and leave me adrift on the dive and bugger off back to shore. I put my dive bag in the back of their truck and off we went, making small talk as we went. After an hour, we arrived at the departure point.

There were close to 30 other divers stood around, all from different countries. After some organised chaos, we stepped aboard the boat and I found a place to sit, stowing my dive bag under the seat just to keep an eye on it. As more and more people climbed aboard, it looked a lot like a refugee boat. People everywhere, all speaking in different languages and packed in like sardines, the engine coughed in to life and off we chugged. There was no wheel house and I looked around to see how and who was steering the boat. There he was, a young man about 20, poking out from the deck with just his head and shoulders to be seen above the deck. That was a new one on me, but he seemed to know what he was doing and we were on site in just 20 minutes.

Kitting up didn't take long, a 5 mil shorty wetsuit, a single 12 litre cylinder, weight belt, fins and a mask. It took all of 5 minutes and I was ready to dive. The shop owner came over and introduced me and 12 other people to the dive instructor who was going to act as a guide on this dive. He had a 15 litre tank and gave a very brief dive plan to us. Basically, he said when anyone gets to 5 minutes deco, or 50 bar, they should make their way back to the shot line and that was that, we were over the side and in the water. I dipped my head under the surface and there she was, this massive ferry lying on her side, just 18 metres from the surface, in clear, Mediterranean warm, blue water. It felt good to be just in a thin wetsuit and basic dive gear. Drysuits and multi cylinders have their benefits and advantages on cold, deep dives back in the UK, but they were not needed today.

The guide joined us and after a quick check, we all dropped down the shot line, finning across the guide rail and down the gang way. I took the opportunity to snap some shots before I dropped down to the lorry deck, where I was suitably impressed with a Volvo 38 tonne tractor unit hanging on it's side from a wall that was once a deck. The chains that held it there looked taut and would one day lose their grip on the truck, but hopefully not today. The guide finned over to one of the wheels and pushed the tyre valve on the front tyre and demonstrated how to breathe off the air that escaped from the tyre. Quite impressive, but I bet it tasted stale and rubbery; he would have been better off keeping his regulator in his mouth. Just PADI party tricks. Just then, a huge Grouper came to join us, it's curiosity bringing it very close to us. Reaching out, I touched it's tail and it didn't even notice. It was now hovering with it's large mouth open just in front of the guide; he had produced some hard boiled eggs.

As he released one, the Grouper sucked it in to its mouth and it was gone. He did the same with another, but this time he broke it up and hoards of small fish joined in on a feeding frenzy, all over a boiled egg. I was so busy watching the performance that I clean forgot to get some pictures and it was time to head off to a different part of this massive wreck. More vehicles were chained to vertical walls. It was bizarre to see the windows closed, with just a thin layer of algae on them, tyres fully inflated and trailers ready to roll, but only for deep sea truckers these days.

I checked my air; 60 bar, time to head back in sight of the shot line for me. I gave the guide a signal and made my way to the shot line, so with just under 50 bar and 4 minutes deco, I made my way up it. At 8 metres, I stopped and waited to see where the others were and to start my deco. The guide was rounding up the other divers and pointing them back to the shot line. Two came back and no sooner had they started to ascend than they went shooting to the surface. The guide saw it and was making arm gestures for them to come back down, but they did not respond. He then got the rest of the stragglers back on the line and just as he joined them coming up the line, two of the divers just let go of the shot line and headed back down to the wreck. With that, the guide chased after them and at that point, I had to admit, I was diving with a bunch of crazy buggers. After 5 minutes he had caught these two and they were back on the line. I finished my deco and made my way to the surface and the sanity of the boat. I climbed back aboard and de kitted, soaking up the sun as I quenched my thirst and waited for the show down when the guide got back on board. As soon as he had placed one foot on deck, he took the two rapid ascent divers to task and then the other two. All they did was raise their hands and made like they couldn't help it. These were perfect diving conditions. If they ever dived in the UK, they would probably kill themselves.

I had my own thoughts on the recent events and so did the guide, along with every other diver on the boat, but as I was the only Brit and they all spoke in their own language, I could only guess. The way they were talking, I think they could have written a paperback called The Book of Excuses. Personally, I had a great dive and like most dives abroad, they are usually a bit disorganised, filled with random people that shouldn't have a snorkel certificate, let alone a diving certificate. I always pick my dive buddies with care; you tend to live longer that way. It's not the environment to act like a clown ass.

With the right dive crew it would be great to have dived inside it. These days, there are some well known swim throughs, although people have still lost their way inside her and have paid with their lives. Maybe I will get back there one day, but until then, I will just have to make do with my memories, photographs and the lure of other great wrecks in exotic places.

Throughout the next two years, I continued to dive quality wrecks using Trimix, Nitrox and air, along with overseeing the club dives as Diving Officer at Portway Divers. In that time, I saw club members come and go. I had enjoyed the benefits of a friendly, active dive club, joining in some major club projects like building a permanent boat house and a new dive boat.

Blue Springs Florida

In 1999, I was in America on holiday and my brother was living in Florida. I met up with him and at 6 am, we set off to meet up with a local diver who was going to take me down to dive Blue Springs just outside Daytona Beach .The springs were set inside a national park. The water from the spring flowed in to a small river that in turn flowed in to the St Johns River. Manatees, long nose fish and alligators were the main inhabitants, little did I know.

We loaded the dive gear in to the pick up truck and set off with the cool morning air and mist just rising from the Everglades. My new dive buddies were a Puertorican man and his daughter. They were PADI trained and had been diving for just a few years, but had a knowledge of the springs. Arriving at the national park, we checked in with the ranger at the gate house and after handing over our dive certificates, he came out and searched our dive bags for under water lights and removed them from our dive kit.

I had not been surprised, mainly because I had been told that because neither of us had a cave diving ticket, they would not allow us to penetrate deep in to the spring and this was achieved by not allowing us lights. Clever Ranger.

We parked up and I put my shorty wetsuit on. The humidity and heat were stifling, even keeping under the trees and avoiding the rising sun. There were mosquitoes everywhere and it was now a race to finish kitting up and get down to the water before I either passed out due to the heat or got bitten to death. Oh and mind you don't stand on a fire ant nest or any snakes!

I made it down to the water's edge with just a few extra mozi bites and quickly got myself in to the safety of the water. My dive buddy led the way over to the entry point to the spring. A large, dead tree lay across it and after a few buddy checks we dropped below the surface and entered the limestone cavern and began to fin down. As the light began to fade, my resourceful dive buddy produced two small hand held torches and we were back in business. As I pushed on deeper, the limestone walls became narrower and shaped in to a rippled tunnel. I was finding it harder to go deeper and thought I had lost my weight belt.

Checking my belt, it was still there, but I was now buoyant and as the walls were smooth as glass, there was little to hang on to or pull on. Then it hit me, it was the force of the water pushing me back the way I had come and that was the point I decided to call it a day for this dive. I turned to the others and as soon as we stopped finning, the force of the water forced us back up in to the larger chamber and at 10 metres we were able to rest and take in the splendour of the limestone surroundings we were in.

Taking my camera, I took a few photos and then we made our way back out in to the main river. As I broke the surface, the heat from the sun began to heat up my head within 2 minutes and my new dive buddy suggested we just drift down the river to get closer to the truck, avoiding a long walk back up a hill in the 90 degree heat. It sounded good to me and with no further ado we were off, drifting down the cool river.

With my mask and snorkel floating just on the surface, I could see the river bed and both sides of the bank. There were dead trees, rocks and various size fish, some over 4 feet long, but no Manatees. After just 5 minutes there was a huge splash in the water on my right hand side. It stopped me dead in the water. I shot a glance to my dive buddy who had also stopped, "What the Hell was that?" I asked, "Oh, don't worry it's just an alligator, he won't harm you. You are far too big for him to bother you".

Glancing to my right, just under the surface, there it was, not 8 feet away from me. A bloody 'gator and no, it didn't look like it was after me, but I liked my arms and legs still attached and without further reassurance from my dive buddy, I got the f**k out of the water, scrambling up the opposite bank like someone being chased in the film Deliverance. The buddy carried on down the river a few extra feet just to make a point and then got out. I personally think he had second thoughts himself, but he didn't let on.

Back at the truck, we braved the mossies, heat and snakes, quickly got changed and headed off to Wendy's for some brunch. The dive had been well worth the early start, bites and the brief encounter with the 'gator and as with most great dives, I was thinking how I would top this dive. As it happened, I wouldn't have to wait too long.

The holiday was also great, but fast coming to an end. The past two weeks had flown by and although we hadn't stopped since we arrived, there were still lots of things that we would just not have enough time to do and would have to wait until next time. On the last day, packing my case, I wrapped my camera up in some dive T shirts and hoped that there would be some good photos to remind me of the dive at Blue Springs.

Custodians of the Duke of Buccleuch

Arriving back in the UK, I got a call from my dive buddy, there was a mid week dive booked and there was a space on it for me, if I wanted to go. I checked my workload and decided I could make the Friday and Saturday dives, it just meant I would have to get off work early on the Thursday to travel down to Littlehampton, ready for the dive on the Friday.

After half a day filling my tanks ready for the deep dives ahead, it was time to rush round the dive shop to get them topped off with compressed air and do some chores at home for my sins.

The following week came quickly; I was on my way to Littlehampton. The weather had been hot and sunny all week and from my conversation with Darren the previous evening, the underwater visibility had been excellent and I was looking forward to the diving. My expectations were high. We would be diving the *Duke of Buccleuch*. She was a 3,099 tonne, 4 masted, steam sailing ship, full of Belgian china and glass, all hand painted. She was lying in 65 metres of water and was upright. Her hold contained over 600 tonnes of cargo and could be reached from her deck at 55 metres. After a collision on 7th March 1889, she sank at night with the loss of all 47 crew.

I arrived at Little Hampton just before 5 PM and parked up opposite the marina, stepped out of the car and walked across to the railings overlooking all the boats gently bobbing on the water. The weather had been hot all week and today was no exception, with the temperature just dropping in to the mid seventy's, scanning the various boats it didn't look like the guys were back just yet, I leaned on the railings just taking in the stillness of the day and thinking on the dives I had done just a few weeks ago , then just at the entrance to the marina I spotted our boat with a few familiar faces sat relaxing on the large open back deck, with a quick wave gesture I signalled to them and made my way down to meet them at her birth. After a few introductions I shook hands with Bernie, who was a big fella with hands like shovels. He dived with the others and although I had never met him before, he was a larger than life character and seemed to have plenty of stories to tell. I caught up with the diving they had done that day and reading between the lines it sounded like it had been good. I would be diving with Sally the next day, not my usual buddy, but was assured that she was well qualified and respected within the group that I knew.

We headed out for dinner, a quick bite to eat and an early night it was a 6AM start in the morning and as they say tide and time waits for no man, and we didn't want to be late.

6 AM arriving at the marina, the boat sat still at her mooring with the sun just rising behind it. After 10 minutes, the skipper Paul arrived and we could start to load the dive gear. I had brought twin 12's with a rich Trimix blend that would require a travel mix of 50% Nitrox in a separate 7 litre tank, along with an 80 % Nitrox mix for deco. The dive today was only 50 odd metres and so I had decided to dive on air and save the Trimix for tomorrow. Liz lent me her two empty 12's from her dive the day before and all I needed to do now was get them filled, so it was back to the dive centre.

Whilst the tanks were filled, I headed off to the café for a quick bite of breakfast. There I met Bernie for the first time; he would be joining us today. He was about 50 something and dived with twin 15 litre tanks. He had been diving deep wrecks for years and had more stories to tell than I have had hot dinners. He was quite a character. With breakfast done, I picked up my tanks and headed on back to the boat and we were off to the *Duke*. It was a few hours trip out to the wreck and we all found different ways to pass the time - Bernie had a couple of tins of Stella! The rest of us mortals made do with tea.

The boat was a new fibreglass job with a big open deck at the rear. Loads of room to kit up and we would need it; we would be diving with 4 tanks each and even with only 10 of us on board, the deck was full of dive gear. I had found myself a nice spot up at the bow. The sun was shining and the sea was flat calm. Bernie polished off the first tin and was quickly on to the next. The old boy was as calm and relaxed as someone who was just out for a day of fishing. Me, I was just focusing on the dive ahead, not having dived it before. I could only imagine what lay beneath from what I had heard about her and the rich cargo of fine glass and china lying there just for the taking.

After a lengthy trip out to the wreck site, Paul, the skipper, gave us the low down on where the shot line was and how it was a bit of a way from the wreck. There was a further rope leading off from the shot line at about 48 metres, right on to the wreck. The wreck was lying on it's side and all we needed to do was choose a cargo hatch and dig out some goodies; piece of cake.

I was going to be diving with Sally, as I had mentioned, after a brief introduction with my new buddy and a 20 minute brief on the dive ahead we started kitting up. I had all 4 of my tanks mounted across my back. Sally's were slightly different, 2 on her back with her deco tanks slung under her arms. We were both diving on air with 50 and 80% Nitrox mixes for the lengthy deco we would have to do. Well, time was running and we had better finish kitting up. We would all be going over the side at the same time as we needed to dive during slack water.

Darren and Pete went in first and with a last bit of mask adjustment, we were ready. The skipper Paul shouted "Go!" and I stepped off the platform at the rear of the boat, followed closely by my dive buddy. We reached the marker buoy and dropped beneath the surface and we were on our way. I refrained from putting too much air in to my buoyancy jacket, so that I could reach the wreck quicker. The clock was ticking and we only had a limited amount of time from the moment we left the surface, to the time we had to leave the bottom to commence our decompression stops. The water was clear and at 40 metres, I could see the other rope leading off to the wreck to my right, with the wreck slightly off to the left. It looked fantastic. I could see Darren and Pete already on the wreck I couldn't believe the visibility, it didn't get much better than this.

We left the shot line at 48 metres and followed the other line 50 metres along, then dropped down on to the wreck. Checking my depth, she was just shy of 60 metres according to my dive timer. We finned over to a large open hatch located in the deck. I signalled to Sally and pulled myself in to the opening and started digging around. The silt bellowed up around me and I could feel my breathing rate begin to quicken as I pulled out a pile of plates and loaded them in to my mesh bag. It was half full and I decided to go back just for a few more. It was black as Hell in the hold now and I quickly retrieved another pile and loaded them in the bag.

As I retreated back out of the hold with the bag that was full to the brim with china, my buddy was waiting at the entrance with a helping hand. We dragged the bag across the sea bed away from the wreck and attached it to a lift bag. I took my spare regulator and held it under the bag opening and put some air in. It slowly inflated and it was clear it was going to take quite a bit of air to get this lot off the bottom. I continued to fill the bag and it began to rise. I let it go and just as it started to rise, it plunged back down to the sea bed. We quickly grabbed it and put some more air in it. We couldn't afford to lose this lot and with a big burst of air, it was on it's way to the surface and we were on our way back to the rope. We were a few minutes over our time and had to fin hard to get back to the shot line and to our first deco stop.

We had been at a depth of 60 metres for less than 20 minutes, but our decompression penalties were well over an hour and the current was now starting to run. It was a comfort to be back on the shot line; it made a lengthy decompression a lot more controlled and it got us out of the water a lot quicker with less chance of any problems.

As I ascended, looking back down at the wreck, it looked like a model. You didn't often have visibility this good so when it was there, it paid not to miss it.

As the last of the divers started to make their way back to the shot line, they reminded me of a miniature setting and I was the only person watching them. That's probably because I was a bit narked at this depth, but I had chosen to deny it.

At 18 metres we stopped for the first of many stops. Sally gave me the OK sign and I quickly acknowledged her. I had had the pleasure of diving with lots of different people over the years and a 60 metre dive certainly sorted the men from the boys and for the record she could hold her own with best of them. I would be happy to dive with her again but she was off home the following day, so that would have to wait.

After a while, we were at the 6 metre stop and I was on my 80% Nitrox mix. This would flush out the nitrogen from my body a lot quicker than just air and after 40 minutes we were ready to surface. The sea was still flat calm and the boat was just alongside the buoy. Stepping on to the lift at the rear of the boat, I was glad I didn't have to climb a ladder because after spending nearly 2 hours in the water, the weight on my legs was quite a shock.

We de kitted on the open deck, stowed away the tanks and had a well deserved cup of tea. All the other divers were now back on board and Paul had pulled the anchor and was heading back to port. One of the other divers had unpacked his china and was showing off his 2 hand painted plates. They had a large flower pattern on them. They looked like new and he was well pleased with them. Time to have a look at ours.

I found my bag and pulled the big pile out. They were a mix of white dinner plates and dishes and were decorated with a light blue line around the top edge. Not quite as nice as the flowered ones, but we were well pleased with them and had half each. If I could clean them up a bit, I could eat my tea off them later; or maybe not.

Bernie had some very nice glass. He had dived this wreck a few times and knew just where to look. Each hold had a different cargo and that was the beauty of diving a wreck a few times. Just then, Paul came over to us and had a look, "Very nice", he said "did any of you see the 2 custodians of the wreck?" "No, what do you mean?" I asked. "Well, last week, two divers were lost on the wreck and their bodies are still on her". There was silence while we thought about the scenario of bumping in to these two unfortunate divers that had been down there for over a week.

"Bloody Hell Paul, why didn't you say before the dive?" and after a few minutes Paul replied with a well calculated answer "If I had told you, it would have de focussed you" and I was inclined to agree with him, but I dreaded to think what would have happened if someone, maybe me, had just encountered them out of the blue. Blimey, I could have dropped my china or had a heart attack, but seriously, he probably made the right call, but only because we didn't bump in to them.

We all had our own thoughts on the matter and as I remember, we kept them to ourselves. One thing was sure; it had been a cracking dive. Everyone had some china or glass and there had been no incidents. Text book stuff as I would say. Back at port it was late afternoon and we had tanks to pump ready for tomorrow; it was going to be a deep one.

As the trip back wore on, both of my shoulders began to play up. Skin bends yet again and as usual, I had done nothing wrong, I had even built in a 10% safety margin. It was just one of those things and I would have to live with it. There was no point in telling the others, most of them had seen it all before and after a few hours it would subside a little. Well that was the usual pattern from previous times. If it didn't, it was going to be one uncomfortable night and there was a big dive tomorrow that I didn't want to miss.

The boat slowed as it reached it's mooring and Paul gently guided it alongside the pontoon. As soon as it was tied up, we all swung in to action in getting the empty tanks off. They would need to be filled with various mixes for the deep dive tomorrow. With all the tanks now in a trolley, we pushed it up the pontoon and along to the dive shop.

With the tanks dropped off, we headed to the bunk house for a shower and change of clothes, before heading out for some food. The sun was still hot and we were truly in the height of the British summer. Paul had booked us a table at a local restaurant and would be joining us later for the evening meal. On our way to the restaurant, we selected a pub for a quick drink and piled in. At the bar, whilst ordering the drinks, we spotted a painting of the *Duke* in her hey day. She looked sleek and majestic, cutting through the sea. I was chuffed to have dived her just hours before and would have been happy to dive her again tomorrow and the next day, but there were already dive plans for Saturday.

Ordering a steak, we sat down to share some dive tales and run through the plans for the dive the following day. I would be diving with two other guys and the wreck was in 70 metres. Ah that was a little bit deeper than I had been for a while. There would be no room for error at that depth. My next drink was a coke and an early night back to the bunkhouse.

Back at the bunkhouse, two of the guys revisited lines from the film Zulu, acting out different characters and sketches. It was hilarious & they had it off to a T, even utilising brooms as gun props. Michael Caine as Broomhead, played by Paul, and Stanley Baker as Chard, played by Trevor.

Broomhead: "Fear certainly dries a man's throat, doesn't it? I was never so thirsty in my life."

Chard: "I could have drunk a river."

Broomhead: "Was it like this for you? I mean, how did you feel the first time?"

Chard: "How do you feel?"

Broomhead: "I feel afraid and there's something more, I feel ashamed there. You asked me and I told you how was it your first time."

And other one-liners like:

"Damn the levies man, cowardly men."

"Good show Adendrorff, we'll make an Englishman of you yet."

"Fire at will."

"Who said you could use my men?"

"The army doesn't like more than one disaster in a day. Looks bad in the newspapers and upsets civilians at their breakfast."

It was better than any bedtime story and by 11 o'clock I was in bed sleeping like a baby. I just needed to watch out for those bloody spears, although he didn't actually say that line, but he probably wished he had.

At 6 am, I was up and so were the rest of the gang. Once the tanks had been collected and loaded aboard the boat we dropped in to the café for some breakfast and food provisions for the day. It was going to be a long one; the wreck was in the English Channel and about a 4 hour journey out.

We were away by 8 am and I went about checking my dive kit. I didn't want any surprises before or on the dive. I fitted all my regulators and checked the cylinder pressures and oxygen percentages. Everything was as it should be and there was nothing left to do but chill out, drink plenty of clear liquids and wonder how I was going to get on with the nappy! Well not quite it was an incontinence pair of pants just in case I needed to pee. I would be in the water for close to two and a half hours as there would be some major decompression to do on this dive. I keep telling my self its just in case I need a pee, nothing to do with age or a weak bladder; luckily I wasn't the only one wearing one.

The wreck of the Asger- Ryg

The *Asger- Ryg* was sunk by *U29* on 6th April 1916. She was a 1,380 tonne, iron cargo ship and had just one boiler and a triple expansion engine. I was excited about the dive and a little nervous as well, but on a dive as deep as this it wouldn't pay to be blasé about it.

With 30 minutes to the dive site it was time to get ready. After a quick last pee, I tried my nappy out for size and pulled on my drysuit. I was zipped in to my dry suit, the skipper, lent a hand as we all kitted up. I had the same set up as usual, twin tanks for my bottom mix and two separate tanks for deco. As the bottom mix only had 17% oxygen in it, I would need a travel mix from the surface down to 20 metres, before changing over to my bottom mix.

After some last minute checks, I was ready to dive. Darren and Pete were in the water first along with their underwater scooters. My buddy and I were close behind. We stepped off the back of the boat and disappeared under the clear water of the English Channel. I could just see Darren and Pete disappearing in to the depths on their scooters. The visibility was over 20 metres and I slowed myself down on the shot line ready to do a gas change from my travel mix to my bottom mix. I passed 25 metres and then accelerated my decent. It would take over five minutes to reach the wreck at 70 metres.

As we continued our decent, the visibility was still fantastic and as I fell through the water like a sky diver, deeper and deeper, I listened to the changing noise of the exhaust bubbles from my Poseidon regulator. The gas that flowed in to my lungs was cold and clean tasting, due to the lack of nitrogen and the large amount of helium it took to achieve the mix, but my head was clear as a bell and I was in full control of the dive. I checked my depth gauge and timer, 70 metres.

I shot some more air in to my suit and some in to my buoyancy jacket, so the weight of the tanks was less on my back and we set off towards the wreck. It was unbelievable. Everything was in a grey mono world with just the sound of my exhaust bubbles. I checked my tank pressure and as I took another breath, the gauge needle jumped back from 170 bar. As I exhaled, the needle flicked back up to 169 bar. As I inhaled again, the process repeated itself and the needle only came back up to 168. At this depth I was at extreme pressure and my air consumption was 7 times greater than at the surface. I would need to keep an eye on my gases as it wouldn't pay to run out of gas down there. No one else would be able to spare any of their gas to save you! At that depth you are well and truly on your own.

My dive buddy and I finned off towards the wreck for a closer look and rummage around the large sections of wreckage. I looked towards my right and spotted other divers also rummaging around looking at what looked like part of the paddle wheel. Their bubbles of exhaled gas poured from their regulators. They had formed three streams of small bubbles separated by 5 feet between them. As they exhaled again, they formed another stream of bubbles all making their way upwards to the surface.

We both finned back off to take a better look at the whole wreck. It was awesome, the visibility was over 20 metres, but we had to make our way back to the shot line as we were out of bottom time.

With a final check, I opened my dump valve in my drysuit and started to make my way up the shot line to my first deco stop. This would be one of many, with 3 different gas changes until I reached 6 metres, then I would switch to an 80% Nitrox mix for the final and longest stop of 60 minutes.

I attached myself to the shot line and settled in for the long wait. Some people passed the time by reading. I had not brought a book, but I did have a carton of Ribena. After pulling it free from my pocket, I fumbled for a while with the plastic straw, but eventually succeeded in getting it in to the carton. Then, with the coordination and skill of a surgeon, I managed to get the straw in to my mouth and gulp down the cool drink, eventually passing it to my buddy. Then it was back to just hanging around and checking the dive timer to see how much longer I had to wait.

I only had 20 minutes left, but I was bursting for a pee, it must be time to try out the nappy. So I tried to relax and empty my bladder, but try as I might it was hopeless. I don't know whether it was mind over matter or what, but I just couldn't do it and now I needed to pee even more than I did before. Checking my time, I only had 10 minutes left. I would just have to hang on and hope my bladder didn't burst. One final check and I was good to go and without hesitation, I made for the surface. The boat was just a few feet away and I was back on deck within a few minutes. I quickly dropped my tanks off my back and got Paul to unzip my drysuit. I was on a mission to get out of the suit and to the toilet without wetting myself. It would be so ironic if this were to happen, oh and not to forget the ribbing I would get from the rest of the dive guys. As it happened, I just made it and God, did it feel good. I guess it takes a bit of practice to go back to using nappies after all these years.

Back on the rear deck, the rest of the divers were de kitting. One of the other guys had a very nice bronze deck cannon. It was about 18 inches long and 5 inches in diameter. As the name states, it would have been mounted somewhere on the deck, probably used for signalling other ships, or maybe even in anger to repel unwanted guests. Whatever it was used for, it was a great find.

As for me, I had two bad shoulders, great memories, and goodies from the previous day, it would be a bloody long time before I could top these two dives, maybe I never would? One of the other divers had the compass binnacle. That's the thing, when you dive a wreck that no one else has ever dived, all the goodies were still on them. All you had to do was know where to look and they would be there, and they certainly had been today.

Making our way back to port, I breathed down the last of my Nitrox 80% and 50% mixes just to try and ease my shoulders, but it had little effect and I just had to grin and bear it like I had done before. Little did I know it would take nearly a week for them to get back to normal. Back at port, all that was left to do was unload the boat, say some goodbyes and drive home. It had been a truly great diving trip and it would be some years before I would top it.

Take time out to reflect

By 2003 it was clear to me that my body needed a break from diving. It was a difficult decision to have to make, but it needed to be made I was now getting skin bends on nearly every dive and they were taking longer and longer to right themselves.

Reflecting back over the years I had spent diving, from novice to technical diver, I couldn't feel cheated or down hearted. There were some very fond memories of great dives and funny situations, along with a few near misses. Like the first time I mixed Trimix in the garage. Taking a big breath of helium and talking like Donald Duck, I ran from the garage to the house, just to entertain the kids with my squeaky voice. I had just forgotten one crucial thing, helium does not replace the body's need for oxygen and as soon as I was in the house, my head span and I fell to the floor along with my squeaky voice, gasping for air. After a few breaths, normality was restored and there were laughs all round, at my expense I hasten to add.

The homemade torches were also a fond memory. These were with me for a few years and from great engineering came their limitations. This I found out on a dive in Dorothea Quarry over in north Wales. It was a cold day in February 1996. Darren was keen to dive the location. It was chosen for the depth and it would take all day just to drive up and back with only an hour or so for actual diving. I had been there once before and knew what to expect. Travelling along the B roads leading to the quarry the streams and small rivers were frozen and I was not looking forward to bracing the cold once we arrived, but we were divers and it was all for the greater good.

Kitting up, I had twin 15 litre cylinders and 1 deco mix of 80%, along with my trusty homemade dive lights. After finning out to the deepest spot, Darren and I dropped down and entered the cold dark abyss. As we reached 50 metres, there was a dull thud.

I glanced over to my buddy and he made an arm gesture as if to say "What was that?" I did the same. We carried on lights blazing, then all of a sudden, there was an almighty bang and I thought I had lost the top of my head. Every thing went black and I saw a glittering cascade of glass in front of my eyes. My buddy turned to me and with a look of surprise, pointed to my head. I checked my depth with the aid of his lights (65 metres), and I had no lights, time to end the dive. Back at the surface, my once trusted Toshiba torch had exploded and the lamp part at the front was completely blown apart. Hell! Time to get a new torch and it wouldn't be cheap. Or homemade this time.

Fast approaching my 3 year sabbatical from diving as I like to call it, I took to playing acoustic guitar around Bristol in various pubs. It all started many years ago when I was taking guitar lessons and fancied myself as a rock star, but the hard truth of the matter was I was not that committed to it. I would need to put in much more commitment. As my tutor would say, practice, practice, practice. It took rather longer to learn than I had hoped. I practiced over a few years on and off throughout my diving years and gradually got the hang of it. One turning point for me was on a trip up to Oban with Darren, Ian and his girlfriend Dawn.

It was early in the depths of winter and we had decided to drive to Oban and tow the boat up there as well. We all met up at Ian's place at Tintern. We would go up overnight taking it in turns to drive. There was just one technical issue, the van a short wheel base Transit, only had 3 seats in the front and the back was full to the brim with dive kit, clothes and various other stuff. There was a small space behind the rear doors, just big enough to accommodate one person. It was so small, the person had to lie across the floor, and once the rear doors were shut, it was somewhat claustrophobic. Well it would have been, if you could have seen anything.

After a fine fry up cooked by Dawn, we climbed aboard the van. I got to try out the back of the van first and even managed to get some sleep. Ian took the first driving stint. After 4 hours, the van slowed down and stopped. I was just waking when the rear doors swung open and Ian, Dawn and Darren stood looking at me. "How was it in there?" they asked, with big smiles all round. I had to admit, it wasn't half bad, for the back of a Transit van.

We refuelled and got something to eat and it was back on the road. Ian and Dawn jumped in the back this time and I can only say it looked very cosy, which I am sure they took full advantage of. I got in the driver's seat and set off. The weather was getting colder the further north we went and just outside Glasgow, the first snow fell. I looked at Darren and we both agreed it would be bad if we got stuck in snow, it could mess the whole weekend up! As we pushed on through Loch Lomond, it petered out, much to our relief and by 4 am we were at the caravan park we had booked for the 3 day stay. The only problem was it didn't open until 8 am and the weather was freezing. It was a bit cramped with all 4 of us squashed in the front cab trying to keep warm. We sat it out until 6 am and then we sent Dawn to knock up the campsite people to let us get booked in to our cabin. Dawn was selected because she would get the sympathy vote and would receive the least verbal if they were not amused at the early start to their day. As it happened, they were as good as gold and by 6.30 am we were in. After a cup of tea and with every heater switched on, we all hit the sack for some well deserved sleep.

The alarm woke me from a deep sleep. It was 12 noon and we had some diving to do on the wreck of the *Breada*. We drove to the slip way and had a look around. We were the only people there and it was bitter cold, with a strong wind blowing across the water. We all kitted up and loaded the dive cylinders in the boat and set out to the wreck. As we sped across the wide expanse of water, the rain hit our faces like gravel and after just

5 minutes, we had to drop the speed and cover our faces for fear of losing our skin.

As luck would have it, as we approached the wreck, we could see she was marked with a buoy and we tied our boat off on it. I then got fully kitted up, but just as I turned on my air, I noticed I had not fitted my drysuit inflation hose. I would not be able to put air in the suit as I descended. I knew that there would be some discomfort as the pressure increased the deeper I went, but I only had two options: abort the dive or wing it, and hope the squeeze from the suit wouldn't be too bad. With that last thought, I went over the side with Darren and Ian, but at 18 metres, just on top of the wreck, I could hardly move. The suit had become two sizes too small and was cutting me in half. I could pull my neck seal and let in some water equalising the pressure, but the water was only 6 degrees and getting wet was not a good idea. It was clear that something had to be done as I could not carry on the dive like this. Then divine inspiration came to me in the shape of a small air gun that Darren had attached to his regulator first stage. I pushed the end of the gun up my wrist seal, pushed the trigger and hey presto, air flowed in to the suit and normality was restored to my body and suit and the dive continued. There were squat lobsters everywhere and Ian was collecting them in great earnest. By the end of the dive, he had a bag full and some scallops. We would be eating well tonight.

Ascending back up the shot line, the water went from a green colour to a distorted clear. It was like looking through the wrong prescription glasses. It was caused by the fresh water mixing with the salt water and after a few metres, all was back to normal. Once I was back on the boat, the weather continued to deteriorate and I still had a good 30 minute trip back to shore. I kept my mask on and headed back. Dawn was cold as she had been sat in the boat whilst we had been diving. The sooner we all got back and got changed the better.

Dawn cooked up the food and after a good feast and a warm by the fire we were ready for a beer. Darren and I left Dawn and Ian and strolled up to the club house bar. It was warm and friendly and the beer was cold. I had a few pints and a good chat, but the trip up had taken its toll and by 10 pm I headed back for some more sleep.

The next day was Saturday and we planned two dives back on the *Breada*. We were up by 9 am and after a cooked breakfast, we were off, back to the launch site again. Like the previous day, we were the only people there. After launching the boat, we searched for the toilet, but to my dismay it was locked up for the winter. There was nothing to do but improvise. The woods would have to do. So we set off to take care of business. Dawn went one way, and us three in the other direction. We must have looked like three dirty dogs, but needs must.

Back on the wreck, we had her all to ourselves. I managed to acquire some Second World War shaving kits that still had their razor blades in them, but the cold water was taking its toll and we only managed one dive. By the time we got back to the slip way, it was early afternoon and we decided to head back, get showered, changed and eat. It was Saturday and we would be going to the club for a bit of a session.

We entered the bar at 7 ish and it was packed, quite a difference from the previous night. Darren got the first round in and we grabbed a seat. Looking around, there was a small band up on stage. That's good, entertainment I thought, and slipped off to the gents. When I got back to the table, the compare came over to me and with mic in hand, he lent over to me and announced me as a guest singer from Bristol. I tried to explain that my pals were just kidding and that I was not looking to sing that night or any other night for that matter, but he was having none of it and nor were the rest of the punters, so up I got to a rowdy applause. All I could think of singing was Blowing in the Wind and after I murdered it, the band asked me to sing one of my own songs.

They just didn't get it, or maybe they did. I quickly escaped back to my seat and my prankster mates. It was at that point I promised myself that I would learn one song, just in case this opportunity should ever rear it's head again.

It was a great night and my early song seemed to loosen up many other budding singers that evening. We staggered back to our cabin well past midnight, laughing and joking about the events of the night. The next thing, Dawn was on her back in amongst sheep and duck shit that she had slipped on. We just cracked up. As soon as we could stop laughing, we helped Dawn up and Ian complimented her on the amount of duck and sheep shit she had got on his leather coat she was wearing. Never mind Ian, it would wipe off. That's more than can be said about the woods we had been using as a toilet for the last few days, and we all went in to hysterics once more.

The *Empress of India* is where I cut my teeth on diving deep wrecks. It was where most of the new dive kit was tried and tested; homemade lights, my first drysuit, the legendary up line, lifting port holes and lengthy decompression with alternative gasses.

It was deep, dark and challenging and I loved diving it. One year in the late 80s, I booked up several trips out to her, mostly with the same group of divers. That's how committed we all were, no one wanted to miss anything. One particular weekend in August, I set out from Exmouth with the sun just breaking through the morning sky. The boat cut through the glass-like sea on it's way out to the wreck site of the *Empress*. It was a 3 hour journey, so I just chilled out on the stern deck, chatting and drinking tea. Reaching the dive site the water was like glass and the sun was burning down from high in the blue sky. We had a few girls with us, so the wetsuit boys did their best to spare them an eye full, not that they would be bothered much; being nurses they had seen it all before.

Once kitted up my buddy and I stepped off the rear platform in to the glassy sea. I had been out on this wreck dozens of times and I couldn't remember such tranquil conditions. It could have been a dive setting in the Med, not 10 miles out in the Bristol Channel. Dropping down the shot line there were dozens of large compass jelly fish, some over a metre in diameter with a distinctive purple ring running round their domed top. As I passed through them at a depth of 10 metres, I looked up and could see the hull of our boat with all the jelly fish suspended underneath in the crystal clear water. I refocused, looked back down the shot line and could see Rick Ayrton and his then wife, Mary Jane, 10 to 15 feet below. My buddy Derek gave me the OK signal and we continued down the line through the clear water and barrage of Rick's exhaust bubbles, as they shot past us on their way to the surface.

As we reached the upturned hull, it was like landing on the sea bed. I checked my depth gauge, 40 metres. We dropped down over the side and found a large hole that had been cut in to her by previous salvage divers. I took out my line reel and clipped the end of the line to the side of the hole and made my way in. It was like swimming through gin. Once inside, I glanced back to check the exit point. It was clear and visible and I continued in, letting out the line from the reel. After 8 metres, I found myself at another opening and continued in. It became darker and my torch could only cast a small beam on nearby sections of the cavernous depths of this wreck. At that point it was time to make my way back out. Derek and I then made our way back along the outer hull to the shot line and began our ascent back to the surface. At 6 metres, on our last deco stop, I kept an eye on the jelly fish that were all around us. We wouldn't want one of those around our heads spoiling a great dive.

Back on the *Grace*, we de kitted and Maurice the skipper brought us out a hot cup of tea. "How was the dive?" he asked. "Great" we replied, but he could tell by our faces that we had enjoyed it and so did every other diver that day. It was that good, I decided to have lunch and dive her again later in the afternoon. I had 2 hours to kill before I could dive again, so everyone just did their own thing to pass the time. As the sun got hotter and hotter, people began to leave the deck for the cool waters around the dive boat and once one person had made the plunge, the rest of us followed. After 10 minutes, I got out and let the sun warm me up, leaving the others still in the sea.

After 15 minutes, most of us were back on board. The girls were still in the water, swimming around without a care in the world. That is until they climbed back on board and they, well we, noticed that one of them had a see through swimming cossie on. Being gentlemen and divers, we just looked twice before we brought it to her attention and then offered her a towel to protect her modesty, just in case she thought we were lecherous divers. Not us.

With modesty restored, we dived again on the *Empress* that afternoon and it was just as good. My buddy and I swam right along the port side and back up over the stern. It had been a text book dive and one that I personally would remember for years to come. Sea conditions and underwater visibility like we had that day was not common place in the UK and I was fortunate to be out diving when it presented itself. As they say, right place, right time.

OPEN MIC NIGHTS

I played my first song at a bar called Aunties on the triangle at the top of Park Street, Bristol. I knew two songs and had my guitar at the ready. My wife refused to come, so I was on my own. I had had a few drinks to steady my nerves and the compare Greg, put me on late-ish. It all went well and I was hooked. All I had to do was learn some more songs and that was it. My repertoire grew week by week and so did my confidence. I got to know a lot of good people and played many pubs over the years.

After 2 years, Aunties changed hands and many of us started up our own open mic gigs. I ran one at the Kings Arms in Brislington once a month for 18 months. Over that time, it gathered quite a following with some very talented musicians turning up, month in, month out. It all came to an end when the then landlord did a midnight flit and then the pub went down hill and the magic had gone.

After nearly three years of very little diving and lots of guitar playing, I had a need to get back in to diving again. In early January 2006, I met up with the guys from Portway Divers again and we went diving at Vobster quarry in Frome near Bath. There was a frost on the ground and the water temperature was 4 degrees, but I had a new drysuit and was in the right mind to have a fun, successful dive.

The main reason for the new suit was the fact that I had put on a few extra stones and of course the old suit had shrunk a bit. These suits are legendry for shrinking, especially when you leave them in the cupboard for nearly 3 years, you are middle aged and have been playing guitar in pubs around Bristol. It all takes its toll.

After suiting up, I slipped on my new twin 7 litre tanks and waded down to the water with my buddy Steve Weekly. As soon as we got in the water, my Poseidon regulator went in to a massive free flow due to the cold and within a minute there was a huge lump of ice around the first stage, coming off the tanks. I had no choice but to get out of the water and let it melt. After 5 minutes I was back in, but this time I lay in the water with the first stage actually under water before getting my buddy Steve to turn on my air. This time there was no free flow and we were away.

It felt good to be back in the water, although I had had a few dives the year before, but in the clear waters of the Med. As we made our way down in to the depths of the quarry to the sunken boat at 20 metres, the water temperature dropped a few more degrees and after a mere 20 minutes, I was cold and Steve was shivering. His suit had sprung a leak, so we finned over to the tunnel and after a 20 metre swim through, we exited and made our way to the surface for some tea and a bacon roll.

It was simple as that; I was back in to diving. Like riding a bike, you never forget how to do it and at Easter 2006, Steve Newel booked a week's diving on the island of Gozo. I gave my old mate Derek a call to see if he was interested in coming. We hadn't dived together since he moved away when his marriage finished. He replied by email that he was up for it. Great, we paid our deposits and looked forward to the departure date.

Malta 2006

Easter was quite early in the season even for Malta and I decided to take both wetsuits and drysuits, just in case it was cold. When the date arrived we all met up at Bristol airport. We had a large baggage allowance and no one had any problem with baggage weight.

After a 4 hour flight, I arrived at Malta's airport in the early hours of the morning. The air was quite cool and I needed a sweatshirt for the transfer journey over to Gozo. Whilst on the coach, there was a family arguing about whether they were on the right coach and when we arrived at the ferry terminal, they realised they were in the wrong place and had to ask the driver to drop them off on his way back. They argued all the way, so why they didn't ask someone is beyond me, but we all found it amusing.

After the ferry crossing, we transferred to our accommodation. It was just up the hill from the dive school. Derek and I were on the second floor, Bob and Jean were on the third and Adrian was on the top. The building was all stone walls, ceiling and stair case and out back was an unclean swimming pool, but we wouldn't be needing it as we had the whole of the Mediterranean sea to play in. The next stop was the dive school to fill in a few forms and sign up for the week's dive package.

At the school everyone was laid back and friendly. There was a German girl and two guys who would be our guides for the week. Most of the dives would be from land locations and would involve a lot of walking in full dive kit across volcanic rocks and stone cliffs. Although it was only May and it was cool in the mornings, it was in the 70's later in the day.

The water was cool and dry suits were a blessing, but only in the water. Walking over the rocks in full dive kit was hot, hard work and I was sweating like a pig. After the first dive, it was

152

apparent that the rest of the week would be more of the same, walking and hiking all the way. At the end of the first day we arranged to meet up at a recommended restaurant. There were about 28 of us, although we were not all diving, so the evenings were when we all got a chance to meet up and chat.

The diving over there was land based and involved lots of hard work just to get near the water, let alone on the actual dive site. A typical day usually started with a meet at the dive school, followed by a short half hour drive to a coastal location and then a hike down a load of rocks that were sharp enough to shave with. In full dive kit, with the heat of the Mediterranean sun beating down on you, you were sweating like Hell and after just 5 minutes you thought you were going to melt.

Once you had been in the water for 10 minutes you felt almost human again and were ready for the next endurance, the sponsored fin to the final destination that was usually not worth the effort, but we were on holiday and this type of diving was better than a full day work out at a gym. I was hopeful that I would be a bit fitter at the end of the week, if I didn't kill myself through heat exhaustion or over exertion.

We got to dive a cave on one particular day and arriving early up on top of a canyon, our guide took us to the edge and explained how we would swim down the inlet and out in to the sea, then back in to the cave. Looking down at the sheer drop of the canyon, it reminded me of Cheddar Gorge and given the dive entries we had been expected to undertake this week so far, I had a crazy notion that we would be asked to kit up and scramble down the side.

To my relief, he showed us an alternative route, 170 steps down to the water. Bloody Hell, there was not much in it, either way it was going to be hard work and I now needed the loo, the early starts were play havoc with my bowels. I had a dickey tummy and had to rush along the top of the canyon away from the rest of the divers for a bit of privacy. I just made it and squatted down behind a bush before I realised I had no loo roll and had to improvise by ripping out both my track suit pockets. Feeling pretty pleased with myself, I walked back to the others and the guide asked where had I been and when I told him, he held up a loo roll. "Well it's a bit late now" I said, but we all saw the funny side. Loo roll or pockets? Hmm, loo roll any time, track suit pockets are far too expensive for wiping your ass.

After the morning's entertainment, I kitted up and started walking down the steps. It took over 5 minutes and my leg muscles were burning, but I kept going along with the others. Eventually we all reached the bottom. It was cool and the water was shallow at a narrow, beach like entry point. I quickly put my fins on and walked backwards in to the sea. It was a relief just to get the weight off my back and legs. The water was supporting my whole body and I was just floating in the cool sea.

With everyone in the water we set off on a 20 minute swim to get to the cave entrance. I then dived down to 30 metres, just to enter the cave. Once inside, it was up to 10 metres to view the cathedral inside the cave. There was a fantastic blue light emanating from the entry point to the cave and was quite impressive, although I couldn't capture it very well on the camera.

On the way back, I took a more leisurely fin, stopping to look at various underwater creatures and after 45 minutes, I was back at the waters edge. With fins in hand, we all started the long climb back up the steps. After only thirty steps, the dive guide took pity on me and offered to carry my weight belt. Well, I didn't want to hurt his feelings, so I let him carry it.

Back at the top after a few rest breaks, I thanked him and removed a further 8 kilos of lead weights from my jacket. He was surprised and then understood why I was struggling back up the steps. I needed that amount of weight because my drysuit was so buoyant.

That evening at the restaurant, I ordered a fillet steak, medium rare and it was cooked perfectly. Just what you needed after two dives a day on this island, hiking up rocks just to get to the water, then finning 15 minutes to reach each of the dive sites. The next day I would be diving a ferry sunk not far from the rocky shore, so hopefully there wouldn't be such a hike as it was today.

In the morning we made our way down to the school, loaded up the mini buses and headed off to the dive site. After 30 minutes, our guide parked, we got kitted up and then trudged over to the waters edge. The wreck was in 30 odd metres and it was just a 5 minute swim on the surface before we dropped under the water and down on to the wreck.

The wreck was the most impressive I had seen here so far. She was a decommissioned ferry that plied her way from Gozo to Malta. She had been sunk as a dive site, but had sunk in deeper water than originally planned. She was upside down which meant that there was a lot less to see and her heavy engines pulling at their mountings made her unsafe to enter.

Once down on her hull I finned down to her stern to take a look at the prop and rudder. My dive buddy, Derek, was at hand with his trusty camera and took photos of each of us as we swam through the rudder space which made an interesting back drop for an underwater photo. As we made our way back along the featureless hull, the guide decided to head back in to shallower water and once again we were diving on sand and what looked like grass. Back on dry land we were all a bit disappointed at leaving the wreck so soon, just to end up diving on sand. But the guide had his own reasons, mainly not wanting us to get in to deco. If only he knew we had done more deco than he could imagine.

After the dive, we drove back to a small pizza restaurant and our instructor wandered off. The waiter came over and we all ordered a meal and a pint. This proved to be a big mistake. As the food arrived along with the drink, so did our new dive guide Helga, the German girl. We had met her at the school, but she had been working with a different party. She sat down with us and asked us why we weren't diving on the afternoon dive. We all looked at each other and Ian said "But we are", "Oh no you're not" she firmly replied, "you are drinking!" Slightly taken back by her aggressive manner, we pointed out that we were only having the one with our pizza and that we were going to be diving in the afternoon. "Not with me" she replied and at that point, she got up and went off in a big huff.

Twenty minutes later, our old guide came back and normality and reason was restored, but she had the hump with us for the rest of the week. I think she thought she was dealing with children. Apparently, she had just spent two years working on a live aboard. Oh what joy that must have been for all the paying children, just wanting to be adult and dive. Although she did have one saving grace, she was very fit. Well nobody's perfect, hey.

That evening back at the restaurant, I indulged in another great fillet steak; they only cost Five Maltese pounds and weighed in at 12 ounces. I was going to be the size of a house if I wasn't careful, but with the amount of walking and diving, at the end of the day I was starving and a smaller dinner was not an option. Looking down the table, the rest of the gang were also eating big meals. Well, we were on holiday and they were damn good steaks.

At the end of the week, one of our guys had had given nearly every one the dreaded lurgie, even two of the guides had it. Cough, headache and aching all over, most who had it took to their beds and I was relieved to have avoided it along with the rest that were spared. The last day's diving was on a boat just off the coast of Malta on a wrecked fishing boat. We went over the side and finned down to take a closer look. There must have been 30 divers in it, on it and swimming around it, it was like a plague of locusts. Within a minute you found yourself swimming round with a different buddy, having lost the one you started the dive with, but it did make a nice change from shore diving and sandy sea beds. After 15 minutes, our guide headed back over to the shot line and surfaced. I waited in the water for my turn to climb back on board.

When my turn came, I swam to the boat and caught hold of the stern platform and felt an intense burning on the back of my hand. As I looked to see what was causing the pain, there it was; a small jelly fish. I quickly shook it off, but it was too late, my hand swelled up like a marigold glove and the mark it left looked like a birth mark. Back on the boat I peed on it, but it didn't make much difference to the pain. In 27 years of diving it was my first jelly fish sting, I wished I'd worn my gloves.

When I woke on the last day, my hand was hurting like Hell and I felt like shit. I had the lurgie and all I wanted now was to be home and in my bed, but there was a 2 hour transfer ferry crossing and a 4 hour flight. It was not ideal, but that's the way it was, after what seemed like an eternity, I was on the plane and once it was in the air, I reclined my seat and fell fast asleep. The next thing, we were touching down at Bristol, home sweet home.

I had dived in Malta twice now and although the water was crystal clear and warm, there were not many exceptional dive sites, apart from the Blue Hole on the island of Gozo. That is something else, with its 60 metre depth and vast array of marine life in every direction. Even if you were just snorkelling it would be impressive. It's like a giant goldfish bowl.

There must be some major wrecks in and around the islands from the Second World War; it was just a matter of finding the right dive charter that could put you on them. Maybe one day I will get around to researching what's on offer and get back over there. As air travel is so cheap and far flung places so accessible, divers are spoilt for choice and it's sometimes easier just to go to the usual suspects that have been recommended and with that in mind, I was off too.

The Giannis D

In 2008, I took my wife over to Egypt, a surprise holiday booked for June. We would spend the first week on the Nile visiting all the temples in the searing Egyptian heat of 50 degrees. It was one of those holidays that involved getting up at the crack of dawn, boarding a coach and driving miles to various locations to visit the burial places of famous kings and pharaohs. Even getting up and out just as the sun was rising, we were unable to avoid the intense heat of the sun.

Once back on the cruise ship, we took relief from the sun by sitting in the swimming pool at the bow of the ship drinking cold water. Even though all alcoholic drinks were free, it was just too hot to drink it. As the end of the week drew close, we were looking forward to a change in scenery and the cool breeze from the coast of Hurghada.

We set off in convoy across the desert with an armed guard actually in the coach and armed guards in various vehicles spread out in between the other 50 or so coaches. We travelled for hours and hours and we reflected on how safe we were, or weren't. We concluded that we were, so long as no one wanted to hijack us, and that if there was nothing to worry about, then the armed guards wouldn't be there.

We arrived at the hotel and I must say we were impressed. The large, white stone entrance hall led in to a huge domed reception area with life saving air conditioning. After a swift check in, we made our way down to our beach apartment. That too was excellent, with its queen size bed and marble floor. I opened the patio doors and we were on the beach. This was more like it, time for the beach holiday and some diving.

That evening we strolled up to the end of the beach to the dive school. It was shut, but it looked OK and it was just 5 minutes from our apartment with the dive boats moored up alongside the quay. With all this on my door step, the diving was going to be very relaxed and hassle free. All I needed to do was come back tomorrow and get some dives booked up.

We strolled up to breakfast early and enjoyed a light buffet style spread. You could have as much as you liked, but we had the Egyptian tummy trouble and were living off various tablets and less was best when it came to food. After brekkie I left Kay on the beach topping up her tan and walked up to the dive school to see what was on offer.

The Egyptian guys behind the desk were very helpful and couldn't do enough for me. After filling in some forms, I decided on a 4 day dive package, booking Kay on the first one as a snorkel diver. She would be pleased, all day on a boat. I should point out that she is no sailor; I was just hoping the water would not be rough tomorrow or I would be in trouble.

At 8 o'clock in the morning we boarded the dive boat along with 10 other people. Most were divers and one or two were on their first ever dive, and the guides were happy to cater for us all. First stop was on a reef with various depths, the two novices got in first and then the rest of us. As I stepped off the back of the boat and in to the clear water, I couldn't believe the amount of fish, they were everywhere. I descended to 5 metres and waited for the guide who promptly arrived in the form of a large splash in a full wetsuit. These Egyptians must feel the cold, I was just in a five mil shorty and I was as warm as toast.

The dive guide pointed out a drop off to the right and signalled for me and a German chap to leave the group and have a look if we wanted. So off we went, checking out the marine life as we descended down to 40 metres. The water was slightly colder, but just as clear. As we made our way back up the drop off and back to the boat, I could see a large plastic disc dangling from a rope and on it was written the name of our boat. Rather clever as there were several other boats on the reef.

Back on board, Kay had been whisked off by one of the other guides to do some snorkelling on the top of the large reef. After 20 minutes finning around, she surfaced and climbed back on board. When I asked her how it was, I could see from her face that she was well pleased. She had snorkelled a few times in the Med over a sandy beach, but the Red Sea was something else with it's corals and marine life. If the rest of the diving was as good as today I would be very pleased.

In the afternoon we dived a large fishing boat, sitting just outside the harbour. The visibility was not quite as good, but still 10 metres. We swam right through her, checking out all the various rooms. After the silt stirred up, we swam outside and explored the outer hull and superstructure. For a dive in the harbour, it was not bad at all.

The following day we spent doing a lot of nothing, just reading and laying on the beach. It was just what we needed to recharge our batteries after the previous week's trekking around tomb after tomb in the searing sun, although it was well worth it and the guide we had for the various tomb trips was a wealth of knowledge.

The next day I was out on my own diving some more reefs and with camera in hand, I set about capturing everything that moved. There were Lion fish in groups of 5, thousands of orange fish the size of goldfish, Moray eels, Rays and large Grouper. Then without a care in the world, I brushed against some fire coral with my left elbow. It brought me back down to Earth with a start, the burning sensation was quite intense and although I thought it would be better not to rub it, after 10 minutes, I gave in just on the off chance it would ease the discomfort, but it had no effect. The dive continued for nearly an hour and so did the burning, not even the cool water made any difference. My thoughts turned to how it would feel out of the water and I was about to find out.

I showed the guides back on the boat the red marks on my elbow and they confirmed that it was a fire coral injury and basically there was little they could do for me and told me it would wear off in time. Well, it didn't wear off that day or the next, but I made damn sure I was more careful on the next dives. This was a relatively small area, but it didn't lessen the discomfort.

On the boat as we headed back in for the day, I took the opportunity to chat to the German guy, Carlston, and the only other Brit, Ian. They were both keen on diving on some big wrecks and so was I. When we got back to shore we went to tackle the dive school about what was available for us to dive on. At that point we all got the same feeling that they were not really interested in putting themselves out to accommodate this type of diving, but after a bit of negotiation and the opportunity to make some more money out of us, they made some calls and we were booked on a large charter boat 50 odd miles away the following day.

The plan was that I would meet the dive guide at the school at 6 am and we would pick up Carlston and Ian at their hotels on the way. That night I checked all my dive gear, charged up the battery on my camera and had an early night.

At 5.45, I made my way to the dive school and waited and waited. At 6.15 there was still no one else there bar me, then in the distance back towards my apartment, I saw a figure heading towards me waving their arms, it was my wife. I picked up my dive bag and went to meet her. "They're waiting for you at the hotel reception and have called our room to see if you are still diving today" they could only wait 5 minutes for me. I had to make a dash for the hotel reception if I wanted to dive today.

These bloody Egyptians had told me to meet them at the school only 12 hours ago; it must be the language barrier.

After a gentle trot, I reached the reception and jumped aboard a tatty van with seats in it. The German and the other Brit were already on board, "Crikey, we didn't think you were coming" they greeted me. I was sure they thought I had overslept and then to add insult to the whole mess up, the mini bus turned down the hotel road and pulled up outside the bloody dive school. It beggared belief for sure. They collected some dive gear and we were off, driving to who knows where, to collect some other divers. Driving down the 4 lane road, we stopped in the fourth outside lane and the driver got out and ran across the 3 lanes to an apartment building to alert the dive guide who was also coming with us. At that point, myself and the other two looked out the rear windows, just in time to see a petrol tanker charging down the fourth lane towards us. Needless to say, it did eventually change in to the third lane to avoid smashing in to the back of us. The driver then ran back across the 3 lanes and jumped back in the van, followed closely by the other guy he had gone to get. Well, the 3 of us just looked at each other and agreed that these guys were crazy.

After 20 minutes, we stopped at a hotel and were told to get out and put our dive gear in the back of a 4x4 pick up. With the dive gear in the truck, we were transferred to a taxi and would follow it to where the boat was departing from. Without further ado, we got in the car and he raced off down the road; these guys don't hang about. After a further 45 minutes, we arrived at a large marina and were shown our boat. It was a fair size with a sun deck on top and rear deck for kitting up. Inside was a large saloon with tables and a small galley. All in all it looked the dog's bollocks.

There were 20 of us and once the last of the divers were on board, we set off for the 3 hour journey out to the dive site. I chose to dive on Nitrox and was given a disclaimer to fill out and sign. My dive kit was stowed neatly in a rack centrally located near the rear of the deck. After checking that all my dive gear was in full working order, I made my way up to the sun deck to catch some rays. Most of the other divers were German and kept themselves to themselves and to be honest that suited me fine. I was happy just to chill out and doze in the warm sunshine.

My dive buddy for the day was Ian, the other Brit. He too was on Nitrox. Back in the UK he was diving on Trimix, so I thought he should be fine on the dives today. Having dived with many different people over the years, once you have chatted to a diver you have not dived with before, you get a gut feeling about them as to whether you feel comfortable diving with them and I felt fine about this guy.

As we neared the dive site, we had a briefing from our dive guide. We would be diving a wreck called the *SS Carnatic*, built in the 1860s by the Samuda Brothers on the Isle of Dogs, London. She was 294 feet long and weighed 1,776 tons. Powered by a primitive tandem expansion engine and sail, she struggled to make 12 knots. In her day she was a luxury PO passenger mail ship. Leaving Suez on 12th September 1869, she struck a reef at Abu Nuhas. The captain didn't recognise the danger and did not launch the life boats until two days after hitting the reef. When he did give the command to abandon ship as she began to slide beneath the waves, it was a bit late and 31 people lost their lives as she broke in half. The rest were rescued and taken to Shadwan.

She lay undiscovered for over 150 years and now lies in 25 metres at a 45 degree angel. Discovered in 1984, she is covered in marine organisms and is a very colourful dive.

Once we were on site, one of the boat crew jumped over the side with a rope and with just a breath hold, swam down on to the reef and secured our boat to the mooring point specially located on the reef. This stopped any damage occurring to the reef or the wreck as dozens of boats visit the sites all year long.

Once we were all suited up and the boat was secured to the wreck, I stepped off the platform and in to the sea. What a relief the cooling water was to my overheated body .The guide did a full forward somersault as he entered the water, quite a party piece for a reserved Egyptian diver I thought. As I descended down to the wreck, I could see the full size of it. The water visibility was 30 metres at least and I could see some of the other divers disappearing in to the wreck. Our guide took us down to a large entry point and I followed him in and through some large passageways and compartments. We had just passed through the engine room, her boilers and condensers lying sleeping, never to wake. It was fantastic being able to explore this wreck with such ease. My dive buddy was nothing less than I had expected of him and was always just off to my left shoulder all through the dive. Being at an angle, it was slightly disorientating. There were bottles all over the sea bed and bottom of the wreck. The square windows could be made out easily and as I reached the stern, her rudder and prop were clear to see. From the bow we all headed back in to the wreck for a final look at the boilers and then continued on our way back outside the wreck again. One of the dive crew was filming us as we exited the engine room and finned up towards the upper sections of the wreck. There were masses of fish occupying various sections of the wreck and I had even had a large flat fish the size of a dinner plate try and eat my red lens cover that was dangling off my camera. Pipe fish and Moray eels had also made the wreck their home, but I was just visiting and as with all great dives it was time to leave the wreck and head back to the surface. Ascending the shot line, I stole a last look at the wreck; that was what diving was all about.

Back on the boat I did a quick tank change and it was time for lunch, an hour and a half break and then it was back down on a wreck called the *Giannis D*. Like the *SS Carnatic*, the *Giannis D* hit the same coral plateau. She was launched in 1969 and built by Imadari of Japan. She weighed just under 3,000 tons and was over 100 metres long. In April 1983, after an uneventful journey through the blue waters of the Adriatic and with the war in and around the Suez Canal still going on, she entered Egyptian waters where she was checked for arms and was given the all clear to go through the Canal. A few days after, she hit the reef. All personnel were rescued before she sank and now lies in three sections, the deepest in 27 metres and the shallowest in just 6. The guide told us we were in for a treat if we liked wrecks. With my head just under the surface, I could see this big old girl and I did believe I was in for a treat. I followed the guide down to the deck of the wreck where I spotted a large winch still attached to the deck and just ahead of me the bridge beckoned. As I got closer to the bridge, I saw I had been beaten to the spot by a group from another boat. Their bubbles poured out from where the windows were, although the glass had long gone.

Our guide took us right down to the sea bed and stopped outside a hole in the hull. He turned to us and signalled that we could go in if we wanted to. He got the OK from all of us and we followed him in. Although it was dark, beams of light were cutting through the darkness from small holes above us and I was now swimming from room to room exploring the workings of this once fine ship. As I made my way up a deck, the light got brighter and brighter and fish started to congregate in the brighter corners of the various rooms; this was truly a great dive. I continued to rise through the decks and then finally, I found myself exiting the wreck by the smoke stack; how bloody cool was that? To top it off, the guy with the video camera was at hand to capture the moment.

Outside the wreck we all made our way along the hull back to the shot line. Again there were fish everywhere. It was a shame to have to leave, but I had managed to take lots of photos and would remember this one for a long time.

Back on the boat, Ian, Carlston and I had a good old recap on the great dive we had just had. Yes it had taken a bit of arranging and it took over 12 hours to achieve, but it was worth every minute. When I arrived back at the hotel, Kay had booked us a table at the bistro restaurant; well it was our wedding anniversary. The Egyptian chef baked us a cake and brought it out to us, but I think he thought we had just got married, that old language barrier again. After dinner, over a few beers, I showed Kay the photos I had taken on the two dives that day. It had been a great holiday, but we were heading home tomorrow, and were due to hit the road at 5 am to drive back across the desert in convoy again.

We reached Luxor at 12 o'clock and were told that our flight had been delayed by 3 hours and we would not be boarding our flight home until late afternoon. It was not what we wanted to hear. We eventually got to check in where the check in pirates tried to take £200 from me for excess baggage. After some negotiation, I was taken out the back door to a cash machine and brought back in; all after I had been through security check in I hasten to add. I paid the man £65.00 and we were through. These Egyptians would have the shirt off your back given a chance.

Trouble at Scapa Flow

After my rest from deep diving I was back at Scapa Flow, Rob House, then DO at Portway Divers put together a week's diving back at Scapa Flow and I was keen to go. It had been a few years since I had been to Scapa diving these wrecks I had grown to love.

It would be interesting to see how they were fairing after nearly 87 years at the bottom of the sea. Most of the others had not been to Scapa before, but they too were looking forward to checking out the wrecks they had heard so much about from other people. There was a mixed group making up the 11 other divers: Craig, Bob, Steve, Rich, Rob, Martin, Dave, Phil, Steve, Andy, and Sarah. Some of them drove up, while 5 of us, including me, flew from Bristol airport. We met at the airport and after a quick check in and a bacon roll we were through departure and on the plane. After a short flight, we arrived at Edinburgh airport where we had to wait for three hours for the connecting flight and although we had avoided the long drive, we weren't that far ahead of the others that were driving.

Eventually our flight was called and we made our way to the departure gate. After another passport check, we walked out to the small twin engine prop plane. Once aboard I found my seat and sank smugly in to the worn blue leather seat with its chrome ashtrays let in to the arm rests. These would have been very functional back in the day when you could smoke yourself silly, passing the time on a long flight. As the engines started to power up and the black propellers began to turn faster and faster, the noise also grew. It was the first prop plane I had ever been on and it all seemed a bit yester year, along with the cracked blue leather seats and the deep leathery smell the plane had. As we taxied to the take off position, the engines grew even louder as the plane roared down the runway and lifted itself in to the sky. We were airborne and on our way to Kirkwall airport.

The drinks flowed during the short hour flight and I got a good view of the surrounding mountains and coast line as the plane made its way and began to descend ready for landing. Yes, it was that quick. As soon as we landed at the very small airport, we were through customs and in to two taxis heading for Stromness, and our boat *Sunrise*. As we drove up to the mooring, I could see she was still the same old boat I remembered; she just had a new skipper, Dougie.

We unloaded our dive gear and boarded *Sunrise*. Rich and I grabbed our bunks and stowed away our dive gear under the covered forward deck. Within 30 minutes we were sorted. The others that had driven were just arriving on the 2 o'clock ferry. All in all, although we flew, it had still taken over 8 hours, but I was not tired like I would have been if I had driven up, it certainly got the thumbs up from me.

With all aboard, Dougie, the skipper gave us the boat introduction and a brief on the diving plan for the week. It would be diving at 8 am, breakfast, diving again at 12.30, then a quick lunch and back to port for 2 pm. He was running a commercial dive business and he wanted to sort us out and get back to his other business that was removing oil from the wreck of the *Royal Oak*. She was sunk at anchor in the Second World War by a U boat with the loss of 800 crew.

The first dive was on a cruiser, the visibility was not too bad and everyone had an event free dive. This was not destined to last. In the afternoon, we dived a battleship and the visibility was poor. I was diving with Rich and we swam along the higher parts, just where the hull met the deck, so that we had a reference point and could follow where we were going. We did 10 minutes one way and then came back the same way. With poor visibility, I thought it was better to moderate the dive according to the conditions and it worked well for Rich and I, we had a good dive with no surprises. Back on board, some of the others had not been happy about the lack of visibility, but had carried on the dive anyway.

With the first 2 dives completed for the first day, we headed for the pub and began a pool tournament that went on from 3 pm to 8 pm, when we stopped for dinner. Steaks, chips and big hearty meals, by 10 pm I was ready for my bed and left some of the others on a mission. Once in my bunk I drifted off, only to be rudely awakened by the late night revellers banging around above me in the saloon. I had been on this boat many times and this bunch were the noisiest bunch I have ever had the misfortune to share a boat with. They had turned in to a bunch of hyper active children. I must be getting old, it's just a shame my hearing was still good, I prayed that there was a God and that they would all have hangovers the next day. With that thought it eventually fell silent and I got to sleep again.

At 7 am, I was up and took pleasure in making lots of noise as I walked around the saloon getting my breakfast. Craig, Bob and a few others were up. We must have been the ones that hit our bunks early. The conversation started with the drunken rabble that made so much noise the previous night. With that, Phil, Steve and Martin came in to the saloon, they looked terrible. We asked them how they were just to make sure. They confirmed they felt bad and we set about making it as bad as we could for them, banging around bashing cups together and talking about greasy fried breakfast. Revenge is sweet, best served up cold.

We were the first boat out and on site for 8 am and Dougie had picked a battleship in 45 metres for the first dive. There seemed to be mixed enthusiasm amongst the dive crew. I had decided to wait and let some of the others go first, if the visibility was as poor as yesterday, I was happy to pass on the dive. Rob and Phil were first over the side and then Steve and Martin. I was sat with all my kit on ready to dive, I just needed to put my mask on and I was good to go, then Phil and the other 3 divers surfaced and climbed back aboard. Phil and Rob got to the wreck, but it was black as night down there they confirmed. You would have needed a 50 watt torch just to see your gauges. At that point I made up my mind to give it a miss, but a few of the others went for it. Personally, I think if you can't see anything, what's the point, but each to their own.

The afternoon dive was on a cruiser and it was a whole lot better. Due to the lesser depth the visibility was fine and like the day before, we were all finished and in the pub again at 1.30pm.

We would be diving the *F2*, a torpedo boat blown to pieces whilst one of its own torpedoes was being salvaged. Bob and George were diving together, hunting for scallops, lobsters and any other crustations. I had a headache and had sat this dive out, drinking tea in the saloon when I was told that Bob had made a buoyant ascent due to lack of air. He had got carried away looking for lobsters and not realised how much decompression he had knocked up and how little air he had in his tank! Back on board, the skipper put him on pure oxygen and then he was whisked off to the deco station for decompression treatment for the rest of the day. We went for lunch to discuss the morning's events and that's where Fizzy Bob was born. George didn't miss his deco and avoided recompression on this occasion.

Back on the boat I cooked Bob's 2 lobsters and 3 crabs and fed them to everyone that enjoyed those sort of things. After 10 minutes there was nothing left, poor Bob; he wouldn't be very pleased, but it would teach him a lesson; don't ever mess up on a dive and leave vital goodies for your dive buddies to look after for you. Period.

The showers on the boat were still outside, leading off from the saloon. We all got to wash and clean up every night before heading out for something to eat and after 2 dives sweating in a drysuit in June, it was great to get freshened up and clean. That evening I met up with Sarah and the rest of the dive crew in the Flipper Bar. Some of the guys were playing pool and the drinks were again flowing. I had a Vodka Red Bull and so did Sarah, conversation was all engaging and the drinks kept coming. We had a deep dive in the morning on the *James Barrie*, 45 metres and we were running through what DVDs we could watch later after we had eaten, instead of drinking all night. With a quick wink to Steve I said "Let's watch Shower Cam", Sarah bit back with "What's that?" her face shocked and concerned, "Well Sarah, we have had one fitted in the shower, we thought it would be a laugh, didn't you know?" She exclaimed "You can't do that!" "Why not?" I said. "Well you just can't! My dad will kill you!" Yes Sarah, I do believe he would, then we all fell about laughing and tears ran down our faces. You should have seen the relief on her face. Fair play to her, to come away diving with 11 blokes. She went on to join the Navy and I hope we gave her a crash course in the workings of the male mind, probably nothing she didn't already know.

From tears of laughter to tears of despair all in 24 hours, emotions were running high. The morning started like any other. We would be diving the wreck of the *James Barrie* just outside of the flow. Currents would be strong and we would be diving it at slack water at about 8.30 am. We would all need to get in quickly so that the last divers didn't miss the slack water window. I would be diving with Rich and Dave. We went over the side and made for the buoy. Rich dropped down the shot line first, I followed and then Dave. The water was clear and I could see Rich disappearing in to the blue depths below me. As I reached 38 metres, Rich disappeared from sight, just as my weight belt slipped from my waist. I tried to reach the buckle, but it must have twisted round. I decided to head back up the line and try to re secure it, but I had begun to pant and my breathing was anything but calm and relaxed and the weight belt was now hooked just on my lower legs. If I should lose it completely, I would be in big trouble, rocketing to the surface and suffering a burst lung or bend. All I now wanted to do was surface in a controlled manner. As I reached 20 metres, I was met by Dave the last diver, tangled in what can only be described as a bird's nest of rope round his head, tank and neck. He had got caught up in some excess rope from the marker buoy.

He looked calm and I began to untie him; first his neck and then his head. I managed to get most of it off, but there were now coils of floating rope all around us and we were sinking deeper. I let go of the rope for a second to reach my weight belt and saw Dave dropping deeper. I signalled to him to put some air in to his suit, but he just stared back at me and continued to drop in to the deep blue. I was now at 15 metres and he was disappearing out of sight. I made a decision to surface and either sort out my weight belt or summon help. My heart was pounding as I caught hold of the last metre of the shot line and surfaced, holding on tight to the small buoy for dear life. Dave was on the other end of it and if I lost my hold on it we would never be able to find him from the surface. I felt my weight belt slip from my legs and the buoy falling from my hands. I managed a distress wave and grabbed hold of the buoy again as the *Sunrise* began her slow turn back towards me. "Come on!" I shouted, but it was hopeless. With Dave on the other end of the buoy he had continued to descend, pulling the rest of the shot line down with him. As the *Sunrise* came along side me, the buoy I was holding on to was pulled from my hands and shot beneath the surface and disappeared. A sick feeling invaded the pit of my stomach as I climbed the ladder back on to the boat. I was met by concerned faces: Dougie, Sarah, Rob and some others. I quickly explained what had happened and we all thought the worst. The whole deck fell silent for what seemed like a lifetime then someone shouted "Diver up!" It was Dave and Rich and they were swimming to the boat. Dougie brought the *Sunrise* alongside them and they climbed back aboard. I was so glad to see him and so were the rest of the dive crew. Sarah had some tears and I must confess I felt pretty choked up as well. All this had happened in less than 15 minutes, it was a scary incident and nobody felt like diving for the rest of that day, as we all did some deep thinking about what had happened and what could have happened; it was a sobering time.

As we sat and drank a cup of tea, the conversation turned to the morning's events and why he just sank to the bottom and how he had freed himself. He had no explanation to why he had just let himself go to the bottom and only realised the seriousness of the situation when he hit bottom and all the rope joined him in a coiled embrace. Lucky for him he kept his head and Rich returned to the shot line to see where we were and of course he found Dave and helped to free him. Then they both came safely to the surface. Today Dave had used one of his nine lives and we had all been lucky not to have lost a diver. One thing is for sure, I will never forget the vision of Dave floating down and down until he was out of sight, and the sick, numb feeling I had back on the *Sunrise*, while we all waited for something to wake us from the night mare.

The following day our skipper Dougie suggested a wreck called *HMS Opal* just outside of Scapa Flow in 10 metres of water. It had recently been discovered and according to Dougie there were lumps of brass everywhere, but as for a wreck, she was smashed to pieces. He wasn't wrong on either count. Once out on the sea I could see shiny brass lumps everywhere and set about trying to pick them up, but most of them were welded to rocks and remains of the steel plate that had once been a torpedo boat, until she hit a rock at full speed in bad weather and blew herself to bits. Judging by the misshaped brass, smooth and stuck solid to everything in sight, there must have been some serious heat generated when she went.

I found a porthole, but it was stuck fast under a piece of plate and so I moved on and checked out the next object and so on. After 40 minutes, I spotted something shining in the sand and pulled it out. To my surprise it was a brass name plate, 5 inches long and 2 inches wide. Stamped in to it were the words H M T B D Opal Spare Gear For Weir 4 ½ Oil Fuel Pump. I held it in my hand and thought wow, what a nice find. With my bag full of odd bits of brass, I made my way back to the surface and re boarded the dive boat. It was quite funny when we all showed off our various bits of tat, everyone recognised someone else's piece they had looked over and thrown back on to the sea bed. That is except for my name plate. I was asked if I wanted it and of course I did; nice try Rich.

That night we all took time out to reflect on the week's diving; the high points, low points and the damn funny points over a few beers, and the general feeling was that we were all wiser men and women and we should all drink to the last two day's diving and the fact we were all still in the land of the living. The following day we dived one of the block ships called the *Doyle*. She is upright in just 16 metres of water. We dived down to her and found a large hole in the side of her hull. I adjusted my tanks and wriggled through. Once inside, the current dropped to zero and I was suspended in gin clear water. As I finned forward through the decks and bulk heads, it reminded me of the wreck of the Inverlane I dived 20 odd years ago and I remembered how tranquil and excited it made me feel. This was a nice wreck to dive and I took the opportunity to take some photos before everyone stirred up the silt making photos impossible. After 40 minutes the visibility was gone and it was time to head back to the surface.

Everyone had enjoyed the dive and we would be back on a cruiser in the afternoon. We had given up on the battleships because of the visibility. I personally think that the cruisers made for a far better dive with the way they lie and the shallow depth and would be happy just diving one like the *Koln* all week. The beauty of diving just one wreck is that you can familiarise yourself with it and do some progressive penetration in to the depths of the ship, where no one has been for 85 years, and maybe bag some good trinkets.

The last day came and went in a flash. We had certainly had a full week's diving, drinking and scary moments. We were spending the last evening in the Ferry Inn. They had a karaoke night and I knew just the person to lower the tone, our man Steve. He played the guitar a bit and although I had never seen him up on stage, he was a legend in his own drysuit. After 3 hours drinking, he got up on stage and began to add his own personal touch to classics like Bohemian Rhapsody and My Way. The four letter words and filth just kept coming, verse after verse; there was no limit to this man's talent, even the hard, rough locals looked on in disbelief. After 30 minutes we persuaded Steve to get off the stage before the whole pub kicked off and we all had to fight our way out. Once he was off, we soon left; it just seemed the right thing to do.

By the time we got back to Bristol, it was not a moment too soon. We all needed a well deserved rest, these late nights, early starts and drinking sessions were taking their toll on us and what with the build up of nitrogen, we were all yawning in between every word. It had been a good week's diving, as it usually was up in the Flow. A few weeks later I read in a newspaper that a diver found a gold wedding ring inscribed with the name of the man who had worn it. He had been a seaman on the *Opal* and had been lost along with most of the ship's company. It apparently is now on show in the museum, although when I was back up there in 2009 I did not see it.

Rough seas above the *Aeonian Sky*

In between major diving trips, I continued to dive with Portway Dive club around the south west coast. The dives were varied and were sometimes doomed by poor visibility. These I tended to forget, but then sometimes you were just blown away by the wreck and the visibility and those dives kept you on a high for weeks, making up for the bad ones. A year ago, Rob House organised a dive on the *Aeonian Sky*. I had dived this wreck 6 or 7 times and although she is a big ship, every time I have dived her I have only been able to see a small section of her and it has been a bit disappointing, but this time was different. Rob and I descended down the line and at 20 metres we could see the wreck and she was big. We finned down on to her and made our way along large walkways and open decks. I could see nearly 15 metres ahead of me. Rob and I were able to explore different parts and then reform and fin on some more. We had a great dive and made our way back up the shot line to carry out our deco stops. It was certainly a dive to tick all the boxes for any self respecting wreck diver.

I can remember a dive on her some years ago when the sea was rough and we went out on the club boat and the swell got bigger and bigger. By the time we arrived on site, I was feeling sea sick. We tied the painter up to the buoy and Steve and I went over the side first, before I got too sea sick to dive. At 10 metres down I could still feel the up and down motion from the surface and I was about to lose my stomach. I signalled to Steve and we aborted the dive and made our way back up the shot line where we met Rich and his dive buddy along with a further 2 other divers coming down as we passed them. We could feel the top swell getting stronger as we neared the surface; there would be no way we could have carried out a controlled ascent, let alone a decompression stop. As we surfaced right under the dive boat, we backed off a few metres so that we didn't get knocked on the head by the pitching boat. I could see Rexina, Richard's wife, struggling on the boat. She shouted at us to just wait while she secured dive kit inside the boat. At that point I saw my water bottles floating in the sea at the stern of the dive boat and knew there was a problem.

I had my twin set of tanks on my back and so I got Steve to help me off with them whilst we were in the sea. I could see Rex moving up and down the boat as Steve and I struggled with getting my tanks off my back, whilst not becoming separated from the boat in the heavy swell as we were thrown about. After a few minutes free from my tanks, I pulled myself in to the boat. As I went over the inflatable port side of the RIB and slid in to the boat, I was back in the water; the sea was level in the boat with the sea outside the boat.

I quickly pulled Steve aboard along with my tanks and the 3 of us set about taking control of this dangerous situation. The engine was still running and the waves were washing over the stern and in to the boat. We had a pump built in to the hull, but it was no use, we would have needed 20 of them to bail out the water quicker than it was coming in. I unclipped the boat from the buoy that it was attached to and pushed the throttle forward. The water poured out over the top of the transom that the engine was attached to. As we ploughed through the heavy swell and the water emptied from the boat, we gained speed and the boat sat higher and higher in the water. Wow, were we all relieved.

I brought the boat about and put it on a course back to the buoy and shot line attached to the wreck. I checked the fuel situation and it didn't look good, the gauge was bouncing from 0 to quarter full. As we slowed nearing the buoy, a wave swamped the boat again and we were back where we started from 5 minutes previously. I turned the boat around and opened the throttle. The stern dug in to the sea and the bow came high out of the water as the sea poured out of the back of the boat again and we became buoyant. I headed back to the buoy, but this time I just kept the boat moving so we could ride the swell and avoid being swamped for the third time. As we circled round and round waiting for the divers to surface, I expressed my disbelief to Rex as to why the others had firstly carried on and dived in these conditions and secondly why they just left her on her own to look after the boat. All she said was that it had been a good job we had come back up when we did.

The first pair surfaced and I took the boat over to pick them up. Rex and Steve pulled them in and Alex commented on the roughness of the sea and I agreed with him. The last two divers were also now on the surface and we got them back in to the boat pretty quickly. The fuel was by now very low. Rich took his dive gear off and we got going back to port. Rich was a good boat handler and he took it back in, we must have been running on vapour by the time we reached port, more luck than judgment. "We were lucky not to have been rescued at sea today." That was a close call; enough said.

Oban in late September

In September 2007, I had the idea of going to Oban for a long weekend's diving. I had spoken to Puffin Divers and they seemed able to accommodate the sort of diving I wanted to do. And after discussing it with a few of my dive buddies I booked it for 5 of us, but within a week we had a further 7 divers that wanted to come, so with a few more calls to the dive centre we had boat places and a bunk house for 12. Just 10 minutes from Puffin Divers and 5 minutes from the nearest pub in the town, we were set.

I had dived with all 11 divers at some point over the years and everyone was up for it. I would be driving up with my old dive buddy. We would have invited an extra diver to share a lift with us, but by the time Darren filled the car with fifteen 3 litre cylinders, a rebreather and my tanks, there wasn't room for much else. We set off at 10 am and made good time up to Glasgow where Darren took over for the long windy road up through Loch Lomond, that's when I remembered how big the loch was and how long it would take to actually get to Oban, but we pressed on, reminiscing on past dives. We finally arrived at the house at 6.30 pm and most of the others were there, so we grabbed the last large double bedroom and headed out to the pub to get in to the holiday vibe.

Phil, the cow man, had arrived last and it was good to see him, better late than never. Last time I saw him was in Scapa a few years ago, he worked a dairy farm and was quite a laugh. After a few introductions, we were all getting on like old mates, sharing stories and telling jokes at 10-ish, then we walked up to the local curry house. Don't get me wrong, a good curry is great, but for the price of this stuff I could get a T-bone steak back at home, but hey ho, the vote was curry, so in we went. We were the only people in there and the waiters soon moved four tables together and got us seated. I went for a mild Tikka with some lamb naan bread, recommended to me by Darren. It was very nice and washed down with a cool beer, I was full, tired and ready for my bed. Once the bill had been settled we walked the short distance back to the bunk house; we needed to be at the dive centre at 6.30 am in the morning.

With frost on the ground, we unloaded our dive kit and found the changing rooms, well, the corridor opposite the toilets in the same block. This was basic to say the least and I chose to change el fresco, as did most of the other guys. Once I was in my drysuit I felt a lot warmer and wandered off to take my dive kit down to the boat. It was a large RIB with fixed seating and a wheel house. Once all the kit was aboard and everyone was seated, our skipper stepped aboard and we got moving.

We reached the wreck site of the *Breda*. I hadn't dived this one for some years, I was over the side and down on the wreck in just a few minutes. It's quite an impressive wreck and what with my buddy's ability to talk underwater due to the fact he was using a rebreather, made for a good dive exploring various dark sections of the wreck. She was a supply ship in the Second World War and the last time I dived her, I got some goodies off of her, but this time there were none. We finished the dive and made our way up the shot line and re boarded the dive Rib, where we were refreshed with soup and Kit Kats. By 1.30 pm, we were back at the jetty where we made room for the next party of divers booked for the afternoon trip. I had chosen the morning dives so that we would have time to enjoy the warm September afternoons, but by the time we had disembarked, filled our tanks, loaded the cars, driven back to the house and showered in the one bathroom with its one toilet, it was late afternoon and most of us were flagging from the long drive, late night and early start. Most of us laid down just for a power nap that turned in to a two hour sleep, waking just in time to go out to find somewhere to eat, but not bloody curry this time.

The next day we were up at 6 again and were looking forward to diving the wreck of the *Thesis*, an iron built cargo ship. She was built in 1887 and sunk in 1889 and was upright in 32 metres of water.

Me and my buddy made our way in and out of the 51 metre long wreck, him on his rebreather and me with my open circuit twin 7s on my back and a side slung 300 bar, 7 under my right arm. I let my buddy lead the way and he found some nice sections for us to check out. As we penetrated some parts, it was good to still be able to see hazy, greenish openings to the exterior of the wreck. We continued around the wreck for 40 minutes and then it was time to go, our deco was racking up and although Darren had an almost unlimited amount of breathing gas, I didn't, and so we made our way back to the shot line to carry out our decompression stops.

After the dive we decided to have dinner at the house. Steve and Rich had a large bag of scallops and were keen to have me cook up something with them. We all put in a tenner and Darren and I went off to the local Morrison's to check out the steaks. As luck would have it, they had rib eye on offer. I had the butcher cut off 12, inch and a half thick steaks for less than £50. The rest we squandered on fine wine and potatoes and other key ingredients vital to the evening meal. Back at the house, Rich, Chris and Ben cleaned out the scallops, all two buckets of them, and I trimmed up the steaks, peeled the potatoes and prepared the other vegetables ready for cooking later. I had decided to borrow a Rich Barrett recipe I helped him cook a few years ago when we were up at Scapa Flow. Scallop pie as he called it, was simple to make on a boat or in a small kitchen, but it had a deep, rich sophisticated intensity that ate very well on its own or as I hoped, with a damn good steak. Once the scallops were cleaned I fried them in butter, garlic, salt and pepper for a minute on each side and then added some white wine, reduced for a few minutes and finally added a pint of double cream and let it thicken slightly. A squeeze of lemon and a slight bit of seasoning to taste and they were done. I transferred them to an oven proof dish, covered them with creamy mashed potatoes and finished off with a generous helping of Cheddar cheese on top and popped it in the oven to brown.

That evening we all sat around the dining table and settled down to quaff a fine selection of wines leading up to dinner. I had room for just two frying pans on the stove and the steaks were so big that only one per pan was possible. Most of the guys wanted them medium rare, so I managed to knock them out one after the other to the hungry gannets, all in 20 minutes; bon appétit.

On the last day we were off to the Mouth of Mull to dive the *SS Shuna*. She was upright in 32 metres of water and sank in 1913, but had only been discovered in 1992. All her non ferrous metal had been removed, but she still made for a great dive. The journey out took over an hour and it was freezing. Ice had formed on my bobble hat and even on my drysuit. I was now cold, a mist has come down and we were having to reduce speed due to the lack of visibility, which did help a bit with the cold. There were a couple sat against the wheel house and she was looking decidedly cold and unwell. Her partner tried to comfort her, but he too looked unsettled and undecided as to whether he made the right decision in coming out on the dive.

We arrived on site and I kitted up and dropped over the side and down the shot line. The visibility was 15 metres and within a few minutes I had the outline of the wreck in view. There was a large circular opening on the top of the deck and I couldn't resist the opportunity to drop in and explore. As I entered it, I found myself in a room with some machinery in it, wheels, gears and piping. After a few minutes, the silt started invading the space and it signalled my time to leave. Back on the deck, I was reunited with my dive buddy Rob and we headed off along the deck. It was a great dive and we took full advantage of the clear water, poking our noses in to all the nooks and crannies the wreck had to offer. I checked my computer and I was in to deco. I signalled to my buddy and he shot his delayed SMB to the surface. We made our way back up it to our first deco stop. Eight minutes later we were on the surface waiting to be picked up by the boat. The water was flat calm with mist hovering 2 metres above it. I took out my regulator and chatted to Rob. We had both enjoyed the dive a lot. It was a shame we couldn't dive her again, but the tides were not slack again until late evening and we were heading home later that day.

Back on the dive boat, the couple had not dived. She was too cold and he had got his weight wrong and had not been able to dive. The pair of them had spent £70, got up early and given up half their weekend to come on the dive. It had not been a good morning for them; they had paid their money and made their choice, but they would have to make do with the reef dive on our way back if they were going to dive at all today.

On the last dive, I collected scallops and packed them in cold dive gear ready to take home. Once we docked, Darren was waiting for me and we quickly loaded the car and got going. We had a long journey ahead and wanted to get home by 10 pm.

It had been a great long weekend diving and if I were fortunate enough to live up there, I would be making good use of the Puffin Divers shuttle service to great wrecks like the ones we had been diving over the last few days. As always with sports, whether it be skiing, diving or climbing, it is all weather dependant and although you can plan and look at past weather patterns, you just never know for certain. Sometimes you just have to take a gamble or seize a weather window opportunity and go for it. We had achieved just that. Roll on the next one.

Pay up and take your chances on an old tub!

I have organised dozens and dozens of dives over the 28 years I have been diving and at the moment I am just happy diving and enjoying other people's efforts, dive locations and enthusiasm. I recently joined a local dive club and booked myself on a dive trip back up to Scapa Flow. The idea of just paying, turning up and diving was perfect. I had got my lift up with a couple of the members and we would just share the driving and fuel costs. Our accommodation was on a different boat to the one I had always used in the past, but what the Hell, I was just keen to get diving on some quality wrecks and see how they had changed since I first dived them 19 years ago.

The journey up was as long and as soul destroying as usual until we got past Glasgow and in to the magnificent scenery of Scotland. After a few stops on the way, I was driving and we were hoping to make the early ferry at 8 am. I kept my foot down and we checked on to the ferry on time and made the early crossing. As we docked at the port of Stromness, it looked like nothing much had changed and then I spotted our boat, a tatty, green, open decked ex-fishing tub.

I thought it was a bit of bad timing as I boarded her and went to find our bunks under the bow deck, the cleaners were still faffing around and the sheets were missing from the mattresses. We made our way from bunk to bunk, they were all much of a muchness; bloody awful. There was mould everywhere on the mattresses, pillows and ceilings. My buddy said "to hell with this!" and went to get a B&B. I had my sleeping bag and pillow and decided to pick the best and try and spruce it up with some deodorant spray.

The others also chose wisely and we went off to the pub whilst the cleaners did a make over. The general feeling was this boat was a bit of a tub, but we would have to make the best of it, we couldn't all afford to go to a B&B. After a few beers and a fine dinner with the sun shining, we all felt a bit more relaxed.

I didn't know all of the other divers prior to coming on the trip, although most of them knew one another from previous dive days and holidays. Most of them were PADI trained and from various walks of life and with various diving experience levels under their belts. After the evening meal, I retired to my bunk at about 10 pm. Although it was still light, I was ready for some shut eye. Down in my bunk it wasn't as bad as I remembered earlier that afternoon. This was due to the fact it was black as night down there with the light turned out and my clean sleeping bag was on a clean sheet, I climbed into my sleeping bag and was asleep within 5 minutes.

At 7 am, I woke to the sound of bumping around up on the top deck. It must be time to rise and shine and with that thought, I pulled on my under suit and left my bunk and made my way to the deck area, where my dive kit was waiting for me and my pending first dive on the light cruiser *Koln*. I had picked out a dive seat next to the entry point, my twin set was all set up ready to dive with my fins, mask and weight belt just tucked under the seat for easy access, my buddy was next to me and he seemed sorted so I headed off to the galley for breakfast.

The galley was very small even by boat standards and the saloon wasn't much bigger, but it would just have to do. I made myself some toast and a mug of tea and went back out on deck. This was the best part of the boat, it was large and airy and the sun was shining. Kevin, our skipper, was on deck filling the tanks with what ever Nitrox mix we wanted. I had mine filled with a 32%. There were high pressure hoses criss crossing all over the place. Our boat was moored next to another boat and we were using her compressor as ours was broken. Oh.

By the time we were all sorted, we were the last to leave and consequently last to the wreck sight. When we arrived, there were two other boats already diving on her. I had a quick chat with Kev our skipper and we turned to starboard and headed for a different wreck. The *Brummer* was slightly shallower, but it didn't have two other boats diving on her, spoiling the visibility. Graham and I went in first and were on the wreck at 16 metres. He finned off down to the sea bed and I followed closely behind him, he was keen on getting as deep as he could. We checked out some openings and he seemed to be keen on staying at the deepest point as long as he could. As my deco began to rack up, I signalled him to follow me back up the shot line. We carried out our deco and climbed back on board where he asked me why I had wanted to finish the dive so soon. I had no intention of racking up loads of deco just for the sake of it. The best part of these wrecks could be found on the upper sides, rather than on the sea bed, with better visibility and longer bottom time, and I told him so. He seemed OK with this and that was that.

The ship's cook had made us some red pepper and tomato soup for our brunch and it was very nice, just the food for after a dive. Once the first mug was finished, I went back for seconds; well it would have been rude not to. We met up with the other boat, pumped our tanks ready for the afternoon dive on the *Koln* and at 3 pm, we were ready to dive again. We were first over the side and down the shot line. When we reached the port side of her, we swam down to the bow. This for me was the best of the cruisers. Reaching the end, we made our way back along and up the shot line without any deco to carry out and we had still had a good 30 minutes dive time on her.

Back in Stromness, I made arrangements to go out and eat and had booked a table in the pub. The steak was rather over cooked, but it was quick and easy and after dinner, I made my way back to the boat where Kevin the skipper was just finishing off filling the tanks for the morning. We would be diving a battleship, *Kron Prince Wilhelm*, sat in 36 metres and upside down. In the morning, my buddy and I were second pair down and we finned off down to the sea bed to view the big guns that lay out across the sea bed. After 5 minutes we became separated due to the poor visibility and we both carried on the dive and surfaced separately. Not ideal, but we were both experienced divers and capable of diving without holding each others hands.

The afternoon dive was on the wreck of the *Dresden*. My buddy and I jumped in and on reaching the marker buoy, he shouted to me to check my fin and I realised I had lost one. I looked down just in time to see it disappearing in to the depths. I had no option but to get back to the boat and borrow a fin. My buddy teamed up with a few other divers and I sat on deck in full dive kit to wait for the first pair of divers to return, so that I could borrow their fins. After 20 minutes, the first pair were up and I quickly relieved Ian of his fins, only to learn that the buoy was not on the wreck and that Ian had been diving on sand. Kev, the skipper, realised the mistake and dropped me on a different buoy. I was diving solo and I had the wreck all to myself. I finned off down the starboard side and after 10 minutes, reached a German flag floating from the wreck. I took my camera and captured the moment. I must admit, I do like diving on my own; you only have yourself to worry about. I turned and retraced my steps and located the shot line to my right. After checking my dive computer, I saw I had 5 minutes before I had to leave and so I continued in the opposite direction for a few minutes and then back to the shot line for my final ascent. It had been worth losing a fin to have the wreck all to myself. Back on board, the other divers told me they all missed the wreck because a random lobster pot buoy had drifted close to the wreck and the skipper had put everyone on that particular one. As they pulled themselves down it, the divers had pulled it away from the wreck and in doing so, missed the wreck completely.

Back in Stromness I went to the dive shop and invested in a new pair of fins. Ironically, I chose some Jet Fins, as they were the cheapest and I had dived with a pair for 10 years before I bought the ones I had just lost. The following day I would get a reminder of how good they were when I dived the wreck of the *Brummer* and I would leave my buddy to do his own thing.

After breakfast, I kitted up and stepped off the boat in to the water. My buddy carried on down to the wreck and then finned off along the middle section of the deck at about 28 metres. I carried on shooting video as we made our way towards the stern, checking out various hatches and openings. After 15 minutes we made our way back along the port side. I checked my dive computer and I was in to five minutes deco. I signalled my buddy and was surprised that he wanted to go down deeper. I pointed to my computer, but it made no difference to him and so I waved him farewell and made my way to the shot line to carry out my first deco stop. Back on deck, the other divers asked on the whereabouts of my dive buddy and I told them he had decided to do his own thing. They were not impressed and quite concerned when he had still not surfaced as I had been back on deck for over 5 minutes. Just then a delayed SMB popped up and we knew it was him.

After just a few moments he made his way to the boat. He sat down and de kitted and then confessed that he had missed 17 minutes deco due to the fact he had forgotten his pony deco tank. He then made it clear he wanted to dive as long as he could, that I was cutting our dives short and he had wanted to dive with a different dive buddy. Personally, I couldn't have agreed more. If I chose to do something daft I am quite sure I could manage it all by myself, and was not about to start it today at least!

Pulling in to port, Kev called me up in to the wheel house and told me that a diver had found my lost fin. 'Well how about that', I thought, the odds of finding it were huge. I walked round and collected it from the diver and gave him a drink for finding it, so now I had a spare set of fins just in case I ever lost one again.

My ex-buddy got his new dive buddy and borrowed a spare dive computer from me as his had gone in to error mode because of the stops he missed on that dive, but he was fine and it was his decision. God knows what would have been said if he had got a bend or something. His new dive buddy worked out fine and I too got a new buddy, simple as that.

The evenings were mainly spent in the Ferry Inn. The weather was 27 degrees, bloody hot for Orkney standards and most of the locals were praying for cloud and rain. As sun lovers, we were enjoying every minute of it, just sat outside chatting and drinking beer. I must say that all the divers in our group were pretty laid back and engaging and we all got along fairly well, even in the close confines of a small dive boat. Everyone adopted a live and let live attitude that suited most people. One sunny afternoon, the dive was planned in Gutter Sound searching for bottles and other tat. I decided not to dive and found myself a coil of ropes up in the bow and had a doze in between reading my book. It was just what I needed. I must be getting old, I thought, and I guess the younger divers would agree. I am certainly not getting any younger that's for sure, but with age comes wisdom. Hold that thought.

On our last day, I got to dive with Greg from the dive shop. We were diving on the *Koln* in the morning and the visibility was nearly 7 metres. As we reached the uppermost side, he signalled me to lead the way and off we went. Greg was at my left side just above me as we made our way to the bow. On reaching it, Greg poked his head in a few open parts of the wreck and I managed to take some photos. As we made our return back to the shot line, Greg resumed his position just above me to my left. I had not had to look for him at any point in the dive, we had both been fully aware of each other's position. He was what I would call a good diver and I would be happy to dive with him any time. Our last dive was on the *Brummer* and the visibility was not brilliant, but down on the bow I could see the deterioration of this once fine wreck. It had collapsed and there were large plates on top of one another. These old wrecks were showing their age, all 90 years in fact. I had certainly seen the best of them over the years I had been diving them.

We loaded up the truck on the Friday afternoon and said goodbye to the divers on our boat that were not leaving until the Saturday and hit the road, it was a long old trip that didn't get any easier, no matter how many times you did it and I don't think I will be doing it again in a hurry.

I had been back for just over 2 months and Rich from the dive club had organised a dive out of West Bay. We would be diving on a wreck called *The Dudley Rose*. She was a dredger sat upside down in 34 metres. We were away from the slip by 9.30 am. On reaching the dive site we were in luck, slack water was early and we could get straight on with the dive. Once all kitted up, Rich and Rex went over the side first and then I followed. I would be using my underwater scooter on the dive and would dive solo. As I reached the shot line, I squeezed the throttle and pointed it downwards. I was now travelling down the shot line and the bow of the wreck soon appeared, standing over 4 metres proud of the sea bed. It was a good start to the dive. Although she was upside down, she was quite intact and there was lots to see. With the aid of the scooter, I got around the wreck twice and I still had plenty of breathing gas and bottom time left. With the visibility still nearly 8 metres or more, I circled round once more and I met up with Rich and Rex. We all left the wreck together and headed back up the shot line; what a great dive.

I coxed the boat back to West Bay and after chips, I headed on home. It was just perfect, on a warm, sunny Sunday in August 2009.

Diving throughout the 28 years has been a journey through the past lives of ships and historical events. It has taken me all over the UK along with some selective overseas trips. I have met many people, strangers at first, but quickly brought together through the common interest in diving. Although I didn't get to dive with all of them, some would leave a lasting memory, some good and some not so good, but one thing was for sure, they all mostly left me with a smile and an amusing thought. As with any sport or activity, it attracts all personalities from various walks of life and sometimes the only thing you have in common is the diving, but happily this isn't the norm.

Just a little uneasy

Walk on trips, when you just pay a dive charter shuttle and turn up on the day and dive, seem to bring out the best and worst in divers. I booked myself on a shuttle out to the wreck of the *Kyarra* out of Swanage. The boat was full and I had no dive buddy. There was another guy also on his own, and he suggested we dive together. I was quite happy to dive on my own and agreed he could tag along with me if he wanted, but if we got separated or he wanted to do something different, then he should carry on by himself and he was OK with this.

We hit the wreck together and as I set off along the deck towards the bow, he was just behind me. After a few minutes, I glanced back and he was out of sight. I waited a few minutes and then he was visible again. I carried on towards the bow and checked out some large openings in the wreck. After a few minutes, I finned back towards him, when I reached him he was just putting his fin back on. He signalled he was OK and I set off again towards the bow. After just a few minutes, I glanced back and lo and behold he was gone again. I waited a few more minutes and a faint light appeared in the distance; he was getting closer, so I resumed my exploration of the wreck, keeping an eye on the distant diver and light. After a further 5 minutes, it had vanished again. I cut short my exploration of the bow and retraced my route back to where I had decended the shot line on to the wreck. After 7 minutes I caught sight of the lone diver, his torch was dim like a dull candle. I gestured for him to follow me in the direction of the shot line and he followed; we had been down just over 17 minutes. I was breathing off twin 7, 300 bar tanks and he had a single 12 litre tank. I checked my air and I had plenty, over 100 bar in each. The visibility was now a bit stirred up and I guessed we were close to the shot line. As we passed it, heading towards the stern, I caught sight of his contents gauge and it didn't look good. I got his attention and he showed me his gauge, yes, he had 30 bar and we were at 28 metres with 2 minutes deco on his computer. I pointed to a rope that looked like the shot line and gestured for him to make for it. Once we had reached it, we ascended, only to find it severed just 5 metres from the wreck. We dropped back down on to the wreck so that we could shoot up a SMB. He unclipped the reel and line from his jacket and I moved in close to use my spare regulator to inflate it. That's when I noticed the wide eyed, panicked look he had. As I put some air in the SMB it raced towards the surface and he was close on its tail. After we reached 15 metres, he was a bit calmer and his gauge read just 15 bars; this was going to be close. With visions of air sharing looming, he got his reel line tangled. We were now at 6 metres and had 3 minutes deco to do. I took the reel from him, gathered the slack nylon line and wrapped it round the reel so that we could do our deco without getting tangled up. Well, we did our deco and surfaced without any air sharing, but he was on empty and it was more luck than planning.

The dive boat came alongside us and I stepped on to the hydraulic platform that lifted me out of the water and on to the deck. I sat down on the bench seat and dropped off my tanks and secured them to the rail. My dive buddy was now backing on board and he got out of his dive gear and sat down next to me. He told me his fin had come off twice and that was why he had lagged behind, then his torch had dimmed due to a lack of battery charging and then he had lost his knife. As for the reel he had not had it long and was still getting used to it. He didn't mention the lack of air, so I asked him why he had let it get so low and that he seemed a bit uneasy down there. He was oblivious to this and dismissed it, like it had been a well planned dive. How can so many things happen to one person in the space of less than 35 minutes? He must have had everyone else's share plus a large slice of the doughnut factor. I hope he learnt a lesson that day, even if he didn't admit anything to me. Divers like that either get their shit together or have a major incident.

There are some tell tell signs to look out for, brand new, shiny kit, hyperactive people and someone that's fiddling with dive kit, either repairing it or trying to understand how it works. Oh yes, and the good old gut feeling.

I once saw someone with a silver drysuit. He looked like someone from Star Trek meets Jacques Cousteau. He had made the suit himself and was full of enthusiasm, but no one would dive with him and so the skipper had to let him dive on his own.

Thankfully most divers I meet these days are either old veterans or divers I don't have to dive with. I have come a long way from when I started diving back in the early 80s with the most basic of dive kit. Depths have gone from 1 metre in the swimming pool to 90 metres in the sea, with every piece of scuba kit I could take in to the water.

Long may the journey last?

My diving has taken me on a journey through life, pushing me forward to achieve greater goals, not just in diving, but in life as a whole. Some of the dives have been truly monumental and others simply fantastic with just a sprinkling of not so good ones, but the good ones always overshadow them. After a bad dive, I always make sure that I get back in the water within a week or two, just to even out the good dive, bad dive balance. Diving, like most adventurous sports, requires planning, the right equipment, the right people and the right frame of mind, and when all these factors come together, it's a winning combination.

Diving, climbing, caving. The list of pursuits are endless but one thing is clear, the people that pursue them do it for the love and passion and only a near death or health problem will stop them doing what they love.

Over the years my dives have been varied and my dive kit has evolved along with my now grey hair. The dives have also been moderated, allowing me to slim down the amount of dive kit, which is good for my back. Most of the dive locations are easier to reach by car and plane these days and there are now various quarries just up the road and fast club ribs to get me out to UK dive sites that much quicker. Flying out to exotic locations, basking in the sun and diving in clear blue waters, well; it's just my idea of a perfect dive holiday. Even the weekend specials I do with the dive club or dive charters within the UK have a great vibe to them. Getting up at 5 am, driving down to the coast on a warm July morning with the sun just on the rise, there is an expectation of excitement about the dive. The journey down, meeting up with fellow divers, the boat trip out to the dive site, it's the whole 9 yards as they say. Even in the depths of winter when it's cold and wet it's still a great buzz.

Earlier this year I dived a wreck off the south west coast near Plymouth. We launched the boat and were away, heading for the wreck site by 9.30 am. After 20 minutes, we were at the dive site. The sea was flat calm and once on the wreck, I found the visibility to be in excess of 15 metres. After the dive, I coxed the dive boat back to Mount Batten slip, the sea was like glass and the sun was shining, the boat was up on the plane doing close on 30 knots when just off to my right at the edge of the bow wave, a dolphin jumped through it. It was so close I could almost touch it. Out of the seven of us that were in the boat, only four of us saw it. It was a shame for them; there one minute and gone the next. Days out like that are just great and it's worth reminding yourself that they don't just happen. Life is no dress rehearsal and as I plan for my 50th birthday and reflect over the past year that I have been writing this book, I can honestly say that it has taken me on a major trip down memory lane, all 27 years of it. Life is not for sitting about daydreaming and sleeping, it's about following your dreams and sharing passions. Loves and passions come in various packages, but I am a firm believer in that everyone should have at least the love and passion for a partner, one for yourself and one for the things you love to do.

Sitting at my PC drawing this last chapter to a close, I am mindful that I will not see out another 28 years diving, but I am sure going to give it my best shot, even if I have to get people to carry my dive kit. Oh, I already do that when I can get away with it! Just remember, you shouldn't get old without getting wiser and with my thoughts wandering to the forth coming dive trip up to the Farne Isles next Wednesday, I think I have it all worked out. Help carrying my kit, a good bunch of mates, a trusty underwater scooter to pull me around underwater and a very understanding wife. Long live the passion for love, life and diving.